SNEAKERS THE COMPLETE LIMITED EDITIONS GUIDE

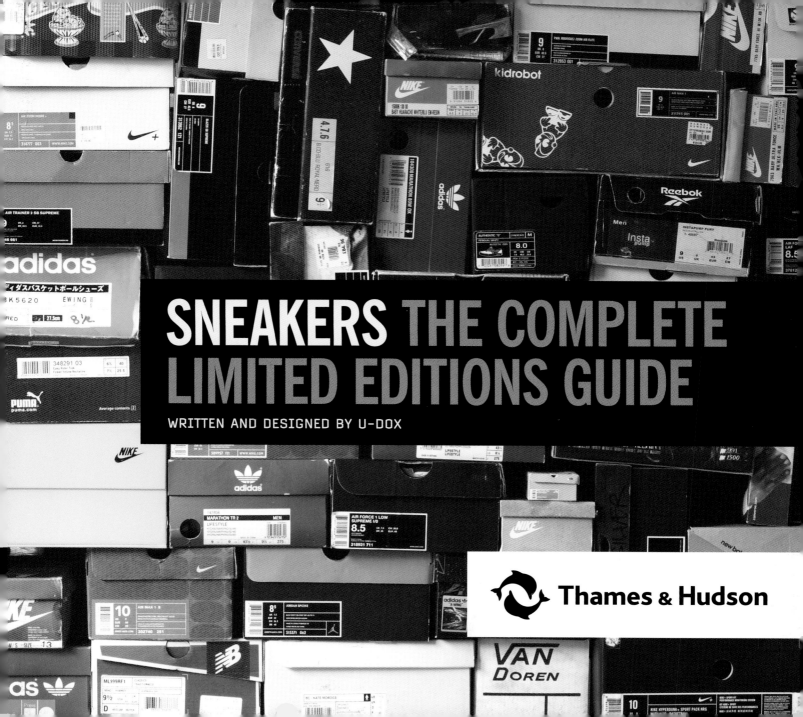

SNEAKERS THE COMPLETE LIMITED EDITIONS GUIDE

WRITTEN AND DESIGNED BY U-DOX

Thames & Hudson

First published in 2014 in hardcover in the United States of America by
Thames & Hudson Inc., 500 Fifth Avenue, New York, New York 10110

thamesandhudsonusa.com

Library of Congress Catalog Card Number 2013947729

ISBN 978-0-500-51728-4

Printed and bound in China by Toppan Leefung Printing Limited

CONTENTS

CONTENTS

INTRODUCTION

Since we published *Sneakers: The Complete Collectors' Guide* back in 2005, sneakers have moved right to the forefront of popular culture, cementing their status as both an everyday fashion staple and the cornerstone of a global, multibillion-dollar industry.

In less than a decade we've witnessed a plethora of sneaker boutiques being opened, websites launched, blogs written, sneaker exhibitions toured and sneaker 'celebrities' born. Athletic footwear has transcended its original purpose and is now worn as a badge of honour across a range of subcultures.

Far from being a localized phenomenon, this growing love for sneakers and the culture surrounding them has quickly spread across the planet. The obsession has been fuelled by technological advancements that make information about, and access

to, any product only a keyboard stroke or screen tap away. Though it was initially fomented in urban centres such as New York, London and Tokyo, today sneaker culture is found everywhere. Even in fairly isolated cities, there are dedicated boutiques where sneakerheads can be seen sleeping out, waiting for the freshest new footwear releases.

The 2005 *Collectors' Guide* was intended to be the complete reference for sneaker enthusiasts or collectors – and, as such, it touched on the burgeoning trend among brands to introduce new interpretations of classic models, often working with creative third parties. Since that time, hundreds of outstanding limited editions and collaborations have hit the shelves, and it is this explosion of creativity that forms the focus of our second volume.

As with the *Collectors' Guide*, it would have been impossible to include here

every limited edition release since 2005 – there has been a non-stop slew of products appearing each year. Our goal had to be to select sneakers that had a global impact – whether they were the most desirable, or the most exclusive.

From one-offs such as the New Balance M576 x House 33 x Crooked Tongues

rulebook and look at new and interesting models of product development. From Nike working with seminal New York graffiti artists Futura (page 147) and Stash (page 134), to adidas creating a new level of product desirability and exclusivity through its work with Japanese streetwear giants A Bathing Ape (pages 20–21), brands have embraced the opportunity to showcase

THERE ARE SIMPLY MANY MORE PEOPLE WHO WANT THESE SNEAKERS THAN THERE ARE PAIRS AVAILABLE

(page 87), to the Nike Air Foamposite One 'Galaxy' (page 139), to adidas ZX 8000 x Jacques Chassaing & Markus Thaler (page 39), we've pulled out some of the key moments in the history of limited editions.

Leading the revolution have been the brands that were willing to tear up the

their sneakers in new ways. In the process, they've opened up avenues to reach new consumers in previously untapped markets.

Along the way, existing sneaker lovers have had their passion for athletic footwear reignited as they have seen their favourite models reissued in new

colourways and materials, often in collaboration with a person they respect.

Obviously, the other crucial element in this equation is the collaborators themselves. They are artists, musicians, taste makers, brand guardians, shop owners, magazine editors, bloggers, blaggers, tattooists, photographers, athletes, designers... the variety is enormous and their number is ever growing.

What they all have in common, though, is a love of sneakers. And being approached by a brand with the chance to tell a story through a piece of footwear, although nowadays a relatively commonplace activity, is still exciting enough that even the most jaded sneakerhead's thoughts will be abuzz with colour blocking and material application possibilities.

Storytelling is also a key part of this phenomenon. With today's consumers ever more engaged and aware, brands need to go even further in an effort to grab their attention and sustain their interest. Initially a bold material make-up and striking colourway were enough, but there has been an unmistakable trend in recent years for designs that attempt to translate something as vague as a 'concept' into sneaker form.

Editions such as the Nike SB 'Pigeon' Dunk (page 149), which references the legendary avian pest of New York City, or the Footpatrol Air Stab (page 132), which riffs on the London public transport upholstery colour scheme, convey a deeper narrative through application of concepts to athletic footwear. The scope for creative interpretation is limitless.

Distribution channels have also changed, and the spread of people interested in sports footwear has grown exponentially. From the thirty-something shoe nerds who reminisce, misty-eyed, about the 'good old days', to the teenagers who are still getting hyped and sleeping out for the latest Air Yeezy (page 154), sneaker culture today really does have something to offer everybody.

Production of these limited collections in such a hungry, knowledgeable and fashion-led market is regulated by one of the most basic economic laws: supply and demand. There are simply many more people who want these sneakers than there are pairs available, and this inspires individuals to go to extreme measures to obtain them, at the same time generating an active resale market with often inflated prices.

People sleep outside stores, scheme, cajole and save for months to obtain that one unobtainable pair. Then they're on to the next one. Once you start to explore the multitude of sneaker forums and websites, or tap into streams of sneaker consciousness on Twitter, the true scale of the obsession in our society becomes clear. It's largely for this reason that we feel now is the time for us to look again at the culture that fascinates and inspires us on a daily basis.

Compiling this second volume has been fun and frustrating in equal measure. From the predictable arguments around which shoes would make the cut, to the challenges of then sourcing some of the rarest sneakers ever produced, it truly has been a labour of love.

We hope you enjoy reading it as much as we did making it.

ADIDAS

With a brand history that reaches all the way back to the first half of the twentieth century, German company adidas has long been at the forefront of athletic footwear and the myriad subcultures it has inspired.

In the late 1980s the groundbreaking collaboration between adidas and Run-DMC spawned an entire sneaker collection. This was one of the first times a brand had made a serious effort to find a new way of marketing sneakers – adidas was arguably a pioneer in forging a strong connection with music, and, in particular, with hip-hop. Check the 'My adidas' Run-DMC Superstar Vintage (page 19) that was released to commemorate the 25th anniversary of the rap outfit's '3-stripes' shout-out in their 1986 song.

Since 2001 adidas has also had a long-standing association with high fashion through its collaboration with Yohji Yamamoto on the Y-3 collection. These forays into working with partners on product collaborations and marketing initiatives stood adidas in good stead for the industry changes that were to come.

In 2003 the brand teamed up with New York sneaker shop Alife for a take on the seminal Top Ten. This low interpretation of the model was featured in our first book as a side-note to the original Top Ten – little did we know that we were looking at the forerunner of an impressive deluge of adidas collaborations that would continue to the present day.

adidas has an unprecedented number of game-changing sneaker models split across its core divisions. The Performance range pushes technological developments, creating footwear that enhances an athlete's actions. Originals are iconic archive silhouettes that are re-released in new and exciting interpretations for people to fall in love with all over again. These releases are often 'tiered'; the highest tier is the Consortium range, which was born of a desire to further explore creative opportunities and sits at the cutting edge of the brand's collaborative projects. The recent Consortium 'B-Sides' shoes were particularly sought after. Not to mention the Style line, which incorporates the SLVR casualwear range.

Over the past decade adidas has collaborated with a wide variety of artists and influencers to produce an impressively diverse range of co-authored sneakers, from whole collections with influential fashion designers such as Jeremy Scott (pages 42–43) under the adidas Originals by Originals (ObyO) umbrella, to executions with some of the key industry players, including Undefeated (pages 12 and 21), Crooked Tongues (pages 13, 27 and 38), Footpatrol (pages 22–23) and A Bathing Ape (pages 20–21). Iconic archive models such as the Campus, Superstar and various members of the ZX family have been reworked numerous times, leading to some interpretations of the originals that are as eye-catching as they are popular.

ADIDAS TOP TEN x UNDEFEATED x ESTEVAN ORIOL '1979'

A TOP TEN TRIUMVIRATE

To celebrate its 1979 basketball design classic, the Top Ten, adidas approached one of the original specialist sneaker stores, Undefeated. The Californian sneaker heavyweights did the silhouette justice by applying a basketball-textured white upper, gold-plated accents and premium leather, all finished with a translucent sole.

To encapsulate the essence of the Top Ten, Undefeated founder James Bond enlisted the skills of photographer Estevan Oriol to put together a coffee-table book based around streetball.

The bound hardback was packaged together with the sneakers in a large black box with hardwood floor interior, limited to 650 units.

SHOE DATA
EDITION
Undefeated x Estevan Oriol '1979'
YEAR RELEASED
2008
ORIGINAL PURPOSE
Basketball
TECHNOLOGY
Pivot point; herringbone sole, padded ankle collar
EXTRAS
Bound photo-essay book curated by Estevan Oriol; specially created box

ADIDAS SUPERSKATE x CROOKED TONGUES

A CROOKED THAI TRADITION

In 2007 the annual BBQ held by online sneaker resource Crooked Tongues took place in Bangkok, Thailand. A series of collaborations commemorated the event, including this adidas Superskate.

Only 300 pairs were made, with particular attention paid to the detailing to ensure that the design reflected the Thai venue.

Keeping the shoe tonal to accentuate its textures, faux elephant skin was used on the 3-Stripes against a rubberized weave, alongside a nubuck and perforated-leather upper that provided more efficient ventilation.

A red silk lining, red suede accents and heel tape bearing the Crooked Tongues mantra, 'Show love and drop knowledge', written in Thai, set the Superskate apart.

This mix of luxury and practicality came enclosed in a Thai-silk Crooked Tongues-branded drawstring bag.

SHOE DATA

EDITION
Crooked Tongues
YEAR RELEASED
2007
ORIGINAL PURPOSE
Skateboarding
TECHNOLOGY
Reinforced layered side panels;
herringbone sole; toe guard
EXTRAS
Silk bag; alternate laces

ADIDAS FORUM MID
ALL-STAR WEEKEND ARIZONA 2009

FORUMS FOR A PRIVILEGED FEW

For the 2009 NBA All-Star Games in Arizona adidas released a very exclusive Forum Mid – this edition was only to be gifted to VIPs at All-Star Weekend.

The make-up featured a combination of mesh, 3M, white leather and snakeskin accents that referenced the Arizona Desert.

The white/burgundy edition represented the West Coast, while a white/navy edition was also released for the East Coast.

SHOE DATA
EDITION
All-Star Weekend Arizona 2009
YEAR RELEASED
2009
ORIGINAL PURPOSE
Basketball
TECHNOLOGY
External heel counter; Criss-cross one-piece ankle bracing system; hook-and-loop ankle strap; pivot point; Multi-disc; Dellinger Web midsole

THE BUTCHER'S BLOCK

Originally released in 1984, the Forum has seen many makeovers, but the original high version has often been overlooked. In 2011 Boston-based designer Frank The Butcher put the shoe back on the map when he teamed up with adidas Portland to create a pack of Forum Hi's true to their original DNA.

Taking inspiration from the hustlers in his home town who wore the Forum Hi during the 90s, Frank wanted to imbue this pair with the same luxury vibe – the shoe was one of the most expensive sneakers on the market at the time (over $100).

Frank's trio of luxurious Forum Hi's featured a tonal nubuck upper, and gold embroidered crests on the ankle and tongue.

The black version shown here was exclusive to Boylston Trading Co. in Boston, while the 'lead' (grey) and 'cardinal' (red) colourways were given to select adidas accounts in the US. None of the three was ever available outside the US.

SHOE DATA

EDITION
Frank The Butcher
PACK
'Crest Pack'
YEAR RELEASED
2011
ORIGINAL PURPOSE
Basketball
TECHNOLOGY
**External heel counter;
Criss-cross one-piece
ankle bracing system;
hook-and-loop ankle
strap; pivot point;
Multi-disc, Dellinger
Web midsole**

ADIDAS SUPERSTAR
'35TH ANNIVERSARY' SERIES

SPECIAL BIRTHDAY TREATMENT FOR AN ICON

To celebrate the Superstar's 35th year, in 2005 adidas released 34 versions of this time-honoured classic, each reworked by partners from the worlds of music and art. The first ever Consortium range also made its debut, in concert with key retailers.

Within five tiers, of which the highest was Consortium, all models in the series were produced in limited numbers. Featured here are the military-inspired

Footpatrol edition (second from bottom left; 300 pairs) and the standout Union edition (bottom left; 400 pairs).

The second-tier Expressions Series featured designs by artists and photographers who applied their talents to Superstars. Graffiti artist Lee Quinones showed his vision by placing images and poetry across the laces (top left; 4,000 pairs). Sam Flores and Ricky Powell of streetwear company Upper Playground went with their love of BBQs (bottom right; 4,000 pairs).

The Music Series embraced the style and lyrics of key musicians linked with the Superstar. Underworld/Tomato conceived a 3M upper featuring lyrics from singer Karl Hyde in an all-over print (centre; 5000 pairs). Stone Roses frontman Ian Brown kept it British with a waxed leather upper (top right; 5,000 pairs).

SHOE DATA

PACK
Superstar '35th Anniversary'
YEAR RELEASED
2005
ORIGINAL PURPOSE
Basketball
TECHNOLOGY
Shell toe; herringbone sole

ADIDAS SUPERSTAR VINTAGE 'TOP SECRET'

BRINGING THE SUPERSTAR BACK TO ITS ROOTS

The final release for the Superstar 35th anniversary series was kept under wraps until it was revealed on 1 April 2005.

Internal craftsmen at adidas – who had worked alongside Adi Dassler back in the day – produced only 300 pairs of this Superstar Vintage. It featured a premium-leather upper and included quality leather shoe-care essentials in the 'Top Secret' combination briefcase.

This premium pack was only gifted to adidas friends and family, or won through a treasure hunt.

SHOE DATA

EDITION
'Top Secret'
PACK
Superstar '35th Anniversary'
YEAR RELEASED
2005
ORIGINAL PURPOSE
Basketball
TECHNOLOGY
Shell toe; herringbone sole
EXTRAS
Leather briefcase; brass shoehorn; shoe polish; x2 shoe brushes; wooden shoehorns; leather tags; dust cloth

ADIDAS SUPERSTAR 80s
x RUN-DMC

25 YEARS OF RUNNING WITH THE DMC

The first ever endorsement deal between a music act and an athletic footwear company started with one song: the infamous 'My adidas', which Run-DMC wrote for their 1986 *Raising Hell* album.

To mark the 25th anniversary of the single, adidas released 1,986 pairs of a special edition Superstar, reflecting the year the record dropped to huge critical and commercial acclaim.

In keeping with classic Run-DMC tradition, the release showcased a black/white colourway on a 1980 Superstar premium-leather upper. Further touches included 'My adidas' tongue tag and lace tips, Run-DMC branded sockliners and a gold rope lace jewel.

SHOE DATA

EDITION
Run-DMC
'25th Anniversary'
YEAR RELEASED
2011
ORIGINAL PURPOSE
Basketball
TECHNOLOGY
Shell toe; herringbone sole
EXTRAS
Alternate coloured laces; lace jewel; special box

ADIDAS SUPERSTAR 80s
'B-SIDES' x A BATHING APE

ANOTHER APE STAR IN THE MAKING

In 2011 adidas Consortium released a special collection dubbed 'B-Sides', based on previously issued rare adidas Originals silhouettes. Two packs were made, with each model mirroring and drawing inspiration from the standout features of its 'A-Side' predecessor.

Easily the most anticipated were the A Bathing Ape Superstar 80s, following on from the 2003 collaboration between adidas and A Bathing Ape (BAPE), which is still highly sought after.

Subtle details included the famous BAPE head debossed into the heel, which was overlaid with a military triple chevron (a nod to the original release that saw the diagonal 3-Stripes striking through the BAPE head logo), and TREFLE EN CHEVRONS ET BAPE diagonally printed on the side panel.

SHOE DATA

EDITION
A Bathing Ape
PACK
'B-Sides'
YEAR RELEASED
2011
ORIGINAL PURPOSE
Basketball
TECHNOLOGY
Shell toe;
herringbone sole

ADIDAS CAMPUS 80s
x A BATHING APE x UNDEFEATED

TRIPLE THREAT

To celebrate adidas' ongoing relationships with A Bathing Ape and Undefeated, the two streetwear labels came together to work on two adidas models of their choice, the Campus 80s and ZX 5000.

Two subtle yet premium versions of the Campus 80s were produced. One featured a black suede upper with a nubuck camouflage-print tongue, lining and insole, with dual branding on the side panel and heeltabs; the other sported an olive suede upper with parallel detailing and a few modifications – the serrated 3-Stripes was replaced with perforations and the tongue was slightly padded out.

The camouflage theme was carried over to the ZX 5000 on the tonal nubuck upper, then offset with the 3-Stripes in contrasting red, white and blue.

The black Campus 80s was sold through BAPE, Undefeated and Consortium partner stores, while the slightly more limited olive version was sold through BAPE, Undefeated and the adidas Concept stores.

SHOE DATA
EDITION
Consortium x BAPE
x Undefeated
YEAR RELEASED
2013
ORIGINAL PURPOSE
Basketball
TECHNOLOGY
Herringbone sole

ADIDAS CAMPUS 80s x FOOTPATROL

THE SHAPE-SHIFTER RETURNS TO ITS 80s ROOTS

For its 2007 collaboration with adidas Originals, Footpatrol re-released the 1980s Campus silhouette, true to its original blueprint after nearly two decades of constant alterations.

The model was slimmed down to its original shape and remade with a luxurious pigskin suede upper in classic Campus colours. The standout feature was the treatment of the medial using a different faux animal skin on each colourway.

Coordinating headbands and wristbands were included, as well as a headshot sticker reminiscent of NBA player Kareem Abdul-Jabbar's signature shoeboxes. The head that embellished this box, however, was that of 2007 Footpatrol store manager Wes Tyerman.

The burgundy, grey and yellow editions were part of the first drop in 2007, while the navy was included in the adidas 'B-Sides' project in 2011.

SHOE DATA
EDITION
'London Olympic'
YEAR RELEASED
2012
ORIGINAL PURPOSE
Running
TECHNOLOGY
Primeknit;
adiZero; Torsion
EXTRAS
Origami-style box;
drawstring bag

ADIDAS **ADIZERO PRIMEKNIT 'LONDON OLYMPIC'**

KNITTING ISN'T JUST FOR GRANNIES

Despite Nike's litigious move against adidas for allegedly infringing its Flyknit patent, adidas moved ahead with the development of the Primeknit range.

This debut version of the innovative, lightweight runner was released on the eve of the London 2012 Olympics, having been produced using breakthrough digital knitting technology that outputs a seamless one-piece upper.

Entirely German-manufactured, the 'London Olympic' edition came in a bright 'Corene red' colourway with white woven 3-Stripes and additional white detailing.

Limited to just 2012 pairs worldwide, each was individually numbered, with the number printed on the box and embroidered on the tongue. The box featured an innovative origami-style opening and came with a drawstring bag.

ADIDAS **SLVR PRIMEKNIT CAMPUS**

KNITTING IS THE NEW BLACK

In 2013 adidas pushed forward with the Primeknit concept, extending the use of the knitting technology from its performance line to its contemporary fashion label, SLVR.

Constructed from a one-piece upper, this Campus's pared-back silhouette was complemented by the textured black-and-white knit, which had a Chevron design. Considered silver details were also featured throughout, on the speckled laces, knitted tongue and the SLVR jewel attached to the top of the tongue.

Each of the 300 pairs was individually numbered.

SHOE DATA

EDITION
SLVR Primeknit
YEAR RELEASED
2013
ORIGINAL PURPOSE
Basketball
TECHNOLOGY
Primeknit

ADIDAS ADICOLOR LO Y1
x TWIST FOR HUF

The adicolor Lo Y1 x Twist for Huf was recalled by adidas after controversy stirred by an illustration on the shoe, drawn by artist Twist (aka Barry McGee). A self-portrait depicting Chinese-American McGee under the guise of 'Ray Fong the bail bondsman' featured him with a bowl haircut, pig nose and buck teeth, enraging Asian-American groups and generating negative media coverage.

The adicolor Lo also featured pinstripes depicting prison bars and innersoles with illustrations of confused detainees.

As the shoe was limited to 1,000 pairs, double boxed with extra laces, lace jewels and a book with Twist's artwork, the product recall ensured the release was even more covetable.

SHOE DATA

EDITION
Consortium – Twist for Huf
PACK
adicolor Project – Yellow/Tier 1
YEAR RELEASED
2006
ORIGINAL PURPOSE
Training shoe
TECHNOLOGY
Ghillie lacing; herringbone sole;
pivot point
EXTRAS
Double boxed; x2 lace jewels;
x4 extra laces; book of Twist artwork

ADIDAS 'OKTOBERFEST'
& 'VIP' MÜNCHEN x CROOKED TONGUES

AN ADIDAS VIP TAKES THE MÜNCHEN HOME

To celebrate Germany's annual Oktoberfest, adidas teamed up with Crooked Tongues to create two interpretations of the München shoe, paying homage to Munich, the home city of the beer festival.

The first colourway utilized elements that were picked out from lederhosen, the traditional Oktoberfest attire. The soft tan leather upper with a perforated toe box for ventilation kept the München easy to wear. Only 300 pairs were made.

adidas's master craftsman, Markus Thaler, designed the second pair. Thaler gave the München a premium outdoor makeover by adding ghillie lace loops and imbued it with a duck boot aesthetic around the toe box. Further touches of Oktoberfest were incorporated with an embroidered edelweiss flower and the Bavarian crest discreetly hidden underneath the tongue. Only 150 pairs were made and they were sold exclusively by Crooked Tongues.

SHOE DATA

EDITION
Crooked Tongues and Markus Thaler
PACK
'Oktoberfest'
YEAR RELEASED
2008
ORIGINAL PURPOSE
Training
TECHNOLOGY
PU sole; pivot point; suction cups; ghillie lacing;
EXTRAS
Pretzel and beer mug hang tag; coaster

SHOE DATA

EDITION
Neighborhood
PACK
'Berlin'
YEAR RELEASED
2006
ORIGINAL PURPOSE
Training
TECHNOLOGY
Vulcanized sole

ADIDAS GAZELLE
'BERLIN' x NEIGHBORHOOD

NEIGHBORHOOD SCORES A WINNER

Japanese streetwear brand Neighborhood joined forces with adidas to celebrate the 2006 FIFA World Cup with this release of the Gazelle 'Berlin', named after the competition final's host city.

The sneakers were available in two versions: one white with black accents and the other a flip of this. Neighborhood's signature skull-and-sword motif featured on the toe box.

The shoes were released on the day of the World Cup Final between Italy and France.

Both designs were extremely rare; the black version was limited to 200 pairs and the white to 300 worldwide.

SHOE DATA
EDITION
Mita Sneakers
YEAR RELEASED
2012
ORIGINAL PURPOSE
Tennis
EXTRAS
Vulcanized sole

ADIDAS ROD LAVER VINTAGE
x MITA SNEAKERS

THE SUM OF ITS PARTS

Mita Sneakers in Tokyo took the slimmed silhouette of the Rod Laver Vintage, integrated it with training classic the Samba, and fused the combination with famed elements of the Campus, a hip-hop favourite, to create a homage to this trio of adidas archive classics.

The result was a suede upper reminiscent of the Campus, while the tongue and outsole featured influences from the cult Samba. The 3-Stripes was represented by subtle perforations, keeping in line with the overall minimal feel of the model.

Signed off with Mita Sneakers' signature wire-fence graphic on the innersole, this was a unique hybrid made with precise attention to detail.

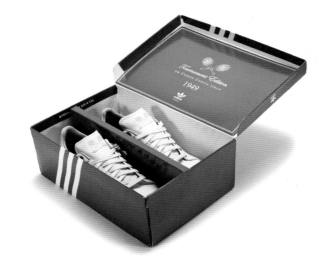

A TALE OF TWO CITIES

No6 in London and sister store No74 in
Berlin are both concept stores built to
showcase premium, limited edition and
one-off products conceived and produced
by adidas.

To celebrate the opening of No74
in 2008, adidas released a special
edition of its Stan Smith Vintage model
as part of the Tournament pack,
a collection that reintroduced the
brand's most famous and sought-after
tennis models to coincide with the
Wimbledon finals.

The silhouette featured a beige canvas
upper, leather lining and foot bed, and
nubuck detailing on the heel tagged with
#74 and #6. Only 150 pairs were sold
exclusively between the two stores.

ADIDAS STAN SMITH VINTAGE
x No74 x No6

SHOE DATA

EDITION
No74 x No6
PACK
'Tournament'
YEAR RELEASED
2008
ORIGINAL PURPOSE
Tennis
EXTRAS
Tournament edition box

ADIDAS ROD LAVER SUPER
x OKI-NI 'NILE CARP FISH'

SHOE DATA

EDITION
oki-ni
PACK
'Nile Carp Fish'
YEAR RELEASED
2005
ORIGINAL PURPOSE
Tennis
TECHNOLOGY
Dual-density
polyurethane sole

SOMETHING SUPER FISHY

This was oki-ni's first ever collaboration with adidas, produced in 2005. The London-based online retailer took an exotic approach to the sneaker design, using real carp fish leather from the Nile in Egypt to construct the upper of the shoe.

The carp leather was dyed in different colours, producing the rusty orange and brown versions pictured here, as well as a blue and a burgundy red. The natural, soft skin is padded out and lined, in Rod Laver Super fashion, while keeping its lightweight dual-density polyurethane sole true to the 80s original.

oki-ni has gone on to produce many more collaborations in conjunction with adidas.

ADIDAS ZX 500 x SHANIQWA JARVIS

MAKING A SPLASH

SHOE DATA

EDITION
Shaniqwa Jarvis
PACK
'Your Story'
YEAR RELEASED
2012
ORIGINAL PURPOSE
Running
TECHNOLOGY
TPU heel counter;
dual-density
EVA midsole;
ghillie lacing

Best known for shooting streetwear impresarios and cultural icons, portrait photographer Shaniqwa Jarvis's wave of inspiration for the Olympics-themed 'Your Story' collection by adidas Consortium came from childhood memories of her local swim team.

Jarvis opted for an interesting mix of suede and neoprene awash with tonal swimming-pool blue. A more technical neoprene was used to construct the tongue, ultimately making it more comfortable to wear.

Further poolside touches included the brown nubuck heeltab that were reminiscent of the walls and tiles of Jarvis's childhood pool, while the dip-dyed yellow, red-tipped laces were suggestive of lane dividers.

ADIDAS ZX 500 x QUOTE

QUOTE SPEAKS UP

For the adidas 'Your Story' project, partners were chosen from various Olympic cities around the world. Representing Berlin was die-hard adidas collector and connoisseur Daniel 'Quote' Kokscht, who produced a ZX 500 influenced by the distinctive blue-and-grey interior of the Olympiastadion.

Quote used a woven nylon mesh and velour trim on the upper, but, rather than applying the breathable open weave mesh to the toe box and tight weave to the side panels, as per the original ZX 500, he switched the two around.

SHOE DATA

EDITION
Quote
PACK
'Your Story'
YEAR RELEASED
2012
ORIGINAL PURPOSE
Running
TECHNOLOGY
TPU heel counter;
dual-density
EVA midsole;
ghillie lacing

GRAFFITI LEGENDS BRING BACK A CLASSIC

The adidas EQT was always a much loved, if seldom seen, running silhouette, but the model returned to the spotlight following this 2007 RMX ('remix') collaboration.

For one of its graffiti-inspired footwear ranges, adidas travelled down a credible route and linked up with the IRAK crew out of New York for this infamous release.

ADIDAS RMX EQT SUPPORT RUNNER x IRAK

The unusually prominent cross-branding is rumoured to have led to the shoe almost being pulled from production. Eventually both the 2007 and 2008 editions dropped online on the same day: 27 December 2007.

These were available exclusively from the Alife Rivington Club in New York and Patta in Amsterdam.

SHOE DATA

EDITION
IRAK
YEAR RELEASED
2007/2008
ORIGINAL PURPOSE
Running
TECHNOLOGY
**Torsion; Soft Cell;
external heel
counter**

ADIDAS ZX 8000 x MITA SNEAKERS

CAN'T GO WRONG KEEPING IT CLASSIC

The adidas ZX 8000 has been instantly recognizable since the original aqua/blue/yellow colourway was released in 1989, with many versions following on from this defining moment in sneaker culture.

The colourway shown here was from a 1991 Equipment (EQT) model. It was first applied to the famous Torsion ZX 8000 back in 2010 as part of the Consortium line, and sold out quickly.

For this version Mita Sneakers switched the colour blocking on the suede-and-mesh upper, swapping white details for black, black for white and changing the tongue from black to grey.

This Japanese Special Make-up (SMU) was also made available to select adidas accounts globally.

SHOE DATA

EDITION
Mita Sneakers
YEAR RELEASED
2013
ORIGINAL PURPOSE
Running
TECHNOLOGY
**Torsion; Soft Cell;
external heel counter;
midsole; ghillie lacing**

ADIDAS SUPERSTAR 1 x STAR WARS '30TH ANNIVERSARY'

FROM DARKNESS SPRINGS LIGHT

To celebrate the 30th anniversary of *Star Wars*, adidas released two pairs of Superstar 1s: a light side inspired by Yoda and a dark inspired by Darth Vader.

The Yoda Superstar featured a mainly hemp upper in imitation of Yoda's robe, with leather detailing on the stripes and heeltab, and a green outsole to represent Yoda's skin. The Darth Vader edition came with a quilted black leather and patent-leather upper in a nod to his helmet and armour.

Both versions were housed in Superstar-branded blister packaging, paying homage to collectable *Star Wars* memorabilia from the past.

The shoes were a part of the adidas Consortium line, only released to stores with a Consortium account.

SHOE DATA

EDITION
Star Wars
PACK
'30th Anniversary'
YEAR RELEASED
2007
ORIGINAL PURPOSE
Basketball
TECHNOLOGY
Herringbone sole;
shell toe
EXTRAS
Extra laces

ADIDAS SUPERSTAR 80s
& ZX 8000 G-SNK x ATMOS

RADIANT REPTILIANS

Beginning in 2009, Tokyo's Atmos collaborated with adidas over several years on a series of five Superstar 80s.

Each pair featured a different coloured upper and various snake scales, ranging from a standard pattern to a python print in G-SNK material – that's glow-in-the-dark – a signature execution that Atmos has since used regularly.

The shoes are highly sought after by collectors, with some pairs more limited in number than others.

Then, in 2011, Atmos reworked the DNA of the legendary ZX 8000 by adding G-SNK material into the mix.

Distribution for the whole series was limited to three stores: No6 in London, No74 in Berlin and Atmos.

The 2012 Superstar model is pictured here.

SHOE DATA

EDITION
Atmos
YEAR RELEASED
2011/2012
ORIGINAL PURPOSE
Basketball; running
TECHNOLOGY
Herringbone sole;
shell toe; Torsion;
Soft Cell; EVA midsole;
external heel counter;
ghillie lacing

ADIDAS ORIGINALS ZX 9000
x CROOKED TONGUES

'T' IS FOR TONGUES

For the 'aZX' project, which featured twenty-six
collaborations on the ZX running series, the letter 'T'
was represented by Crooked Tongues, who opted
to revamp the ZX 9000.

With colour blocking inspired by the mid-90s adidas
ZX range, yellow, grey, carbon and black were
applied on carefully selected materials, an all-suede-
and-mesh combination reminiscent of the original ZX
9000. Further attention to detail could be found on
the innersole, lace jewel, paper packaging and extra
laces, which all carried coordinating artwork designed
by Crooked Tongues affiliate Mark Ward.

Those who bought a pair of these when they dropped
back in 2008 stood the chance of finding a special
pair of gold laces in the box, Willy Wonka-style. The
winner received an exclusive ZX 8000 designed by
adidas stalwarts Jacques Chassaing and Markus
Thaler to commemorate the project.

SHOE DATA
EDITION
Crooked Tongues
PACK
'aZX'
YEAR RELEASED
2008
ORIGINAL PURPOSE
Running
TECHNOLOGY
**Torsion; Soft Cell;
external heel counter;
EVA midsole; ghillie
lacing**
EXTRAS
x4 laces; aZX hang tag

ADIDAS ZX 8000 x JACQUES CHASSAING & MARKUS THALER

THE FINEST QUALITY CONTROL

The ZX series was commemorated in 2008 and 2009 with the launch of 'aZX'. The project's finale came in the shape of the ZX 8000, created by legendary adidas designers Jacques Chassaing and Markus Thaler.

Jacques Chassaing has been a key adidas designer for over thirty years, having worked on many influential adidas models, including all the shoes in the ZX range.

Markus Thaler learnt the tools of the shoemaking trade by working alongside Adi Dassler in the early 70s. He developed some of adidas' most successful technologies, including EQT and the Torsion bar.

Bringing these two great minds together to revisit the ZX 8000 resulted in a handmade, luxurious and premium model, with particular attention paid to the physical construction of the shoe.

Packaged in a large Perspex box with a compartment that broke down the main performance components of the ZX 8000, this is a true collector's piece, with only twenty-two pairs made. One was given to each participating Consortium store.

SHOE DATA

EDITION
Jacques Chassaing
& Markus Thaler
PACK
'aZX'
YEAR RELEASED
2009
ORIGINAL PURPOSE
Running
TECHNOLOGY
Torsion; Soft Cell; EVA
midsole; external heel counter;
ghillie lacing
EXTRAS
Large Perspex box;
deconstructed ZX 8000;
'aZX' hang tag

ADIDAS TRAINING 72 NG
x NOEL GALLAGHER

YOU GOTTA STROLL WITH IT

In October 2011 musician Noel Gallagher collaborated with adidas on one of his favourite models, the Training 72, previously known as the Olympia. The release coincided with that of his debut solo album, *High Flying Birds*.

The sneaker paid tribute to original versions of the Training 72 with adidas blue 3-Stripes, 'Endorsed by Noel Gallagher' branding on the tongue and a brown textured rubber midsole.

They were available in an extremely limited run of 200 pairs worldwide, sold exclusively at No6 in London and No74 in Berlin.

SHOE DATA

EDITION
Training 72 NG
YEAR RELEASED
2011
ORIGINAL PURPOSE
Training
TECHNOLOGY
Herringbone sole;
vulcanized sole
EXTRAS
Noel Gallagher tissue paper

ADIDAS IMMOTILE x BROOKLYN MACHINE WORKS

A MODERN TWIST ON CYCLING HERITAGE

With the explosion of interest in fixed-gear bikes in recent years, there have been some killer models and make-ups aimed at the growing number of cycling enthusiasts. In 2010 this offering for the adidas Consortium range resulted from a collaboration with New York-based cycle originators Brooklyn Machine Works.

The shape and colours of the Immotile were inspired by a seminal Eddy Merckx cycling shoe from the adidas Originals archive. This version kept a similar low profile, but offered a fresh take on the original poppy/silver/aqua colourway.

The combination mesh-and-leather upper provided the perfect blend of durability and breathability, while the lace stay through the tongue ensured a perfect fit for city sojourns. The shoe was finished with an embroidered Brooklyn Machine Works logo on the tongue and lace flip.

The collaboration also spawned an unreleased sample in black with blue detailing.

SHOE DATA
EDITION
Brooklyn Machine Works
YEAR RELEASED
2010
ORIGINAL PURPOSE
Cycling
TECHNOLOGY
Suction cup; pivot point
EXTRAS
Extra laces

ADIDAS JS BEAR x JEREMY SCOTT

PLUSHONISTA: JEREMY'S MAD MENAGERIE

Having previously worked on several products with adidas, in 2010 Jeremy Scott was given the opportunity to be a part of the ObyO (Originals by Originals) range, a top-tier collection by designers and brands such as James Bond from Undefeated and Kazuki Kuraishi.

Scott based his design on the Metro Attitude silhouette, giving it his own unique twist. The upper featured a faux-fur body with a teddy bear head sitting atop the tongue, and arms that were positioned next to the top eyelets. Two colours were originally produced: a pink and a brown version. Multicoloured and camouflage varieties were released a few years later.

The popularity of the teddies spawned a menagerie of Jeremy Scott-designed sneakers, including a panda, leopard, gorilla and poodle.

Much of Scott's ObyO collection is still extremely popular, especially the teddies, which now sell for up to three times their original retail price.

SHOE DATA
EDITION
Teddy Bear
PACK
'ObyO Jeremy Scott'
YEAR RELEASED
2010
ORIGINAL PURPOSE
Basketball
TECHNOLOGY
Dellinger Web midsole

ADIDAS JS WINGS
x **JEREMY SCOTT**

JEREMY GETS IN A FLAP

As a part of flamboyant Jeremy Scott's ongoing work within the adidas ObyO collection, the avant-garde fashion designer dropped this iridescent pair of winged Attitude Hi's as part of his spring/summer 2010 line.

Dubbed the Jeremy Scott 'Rainbow' by many, this version of his classic winged design was an instant attention-grabber with its lenticular material upper, multicoloured eyelets, matching laces and black sole unit.

These are now one of the most sought-after JS Wings ever produced.

SHOE DATA

EDITION
'Rainbow'
PACK
'ObyO Jeremy Scott'
YEAR RELEASED
2010
ORIGINAL PURPOSE
Basketball
TECHNOLOGY
Dellinger Web midsole

ADIDAS SAMBA x LIONEL MESSI

PRIDE OF ARGENTINA

The 'Legacy of Craftsmanship' series gave adidas brand ambassadors their own bespoke pair of Originals silhouettes to enjoy while off-duty. Exchanging ideas between them, master craftsman Markus Thaler and new-school adidas designer Vincent Etcheverry came up with a clean-cut, Argentina-themed adidas Samba for football maestro Lionel Messi.

The sneaker featured precision laser-cut leather panels that were painstakingly glued to the upper, which reduced the number of stitch lines. An Argentinian flag was sewn into the foot bed and 'Messi' featured on the side of the upper.

Only five pairs were produced, all of which were gifted to Messi.

ADIDAS PRO SHELL
x SNOOP DOGG
'SNOOPERSTAR'

SHOE DATA

EDITION
Snoop Dogg
PACK
'Legacy of Craftsmanship'
YEAR RELEASED
2012
ORIGINAL PURPOSE
Basketball
TECHNOLOGY
Hook-and-loop
ankle strap; shell toe;
herringbone sole

SHOE DATA

EDITION
Lionel Messi
PACK
'Legacy of Craftsmanship'
YEAR RELEASED
2012
ORIGINAL PURPOSE
Indoor football training
TECHNOLOGY
Pivot point; suction cup;
laser-cut panels

FROM THE ASHES

Long-time adidas ambassador Snoop Dogg requested a bespoke 'Snooperstar', and so adidas delivered a personalized mid-cut Pro Shell to the rapper, a hybrid of the Superstar and Pro models.

Designer Josh Herr worked with the legendary Markus Thaler, who applied his traditional shoemaking skills. Rastafarian influences were seen on the untreated canvas that was used on the upper instead of the customary leather; the 3-D embroidery on each heel counter represents rising Phoenix wings.

Snoop Dogg's signature was etched onto the midsole, while the label printed on the innersole featured the moniker 'Snooperstar' along with 'Made in France'.

ASICS

Kihachiro Onitsuka founded the Onitsuka Tiger sports shoe company in Japan in 1949. In 1977 the firm became ASICS, and it went on to produce a wide range of athletic footwear and performance equipment for a variety of different sports. These days, ASICS is performance-based, while Onitsuka Tiger lives on as a brand focused mainly on the lifestyle market.

ASICS is an acronym of the Latin *anima sana in corpore sano*, which translates as 'healthy soul in a healthy body', an ethos that the company has kept central to its thinking over the years.

Much of the core athletic footwear range has been designed for running and jogging, and it is the silhouettes associated with these pursuits that have attracted the most attention when adapted for the lifestyle market.

Models such as the Gel Lyte or the cult Gel Saga have seen special editions in recent years that have ensured that the brand remains at the forefront of global sneaker culture. Collaborative partners have queued up for the opportunity to apply their own interpretations to these designs, generally with outstanding and well-received results.

From the early Patta execution of the Gel Lyte (page 59) to the latest instantly sold-out efforts by sneaker designer Ronnie Fieg (pages 49–51), ASICS is a brand that has been re-elevated into the collective awareness of sneaker enthusiasts around the world through its considered approach to limited edition and collaborative projects.

SHOE DATA
EDITION
Mita Sneakers 'Panda'
YEAR RELEASED
2013
ORIGINAL PURPOSE
Basketball
TECHNOLOGY
Sticky sole
EXTRAS
White laces

ONITSUKA TIGER FABRE BL-L
'PANDA' x MITA SNEAKERS

BEAR-FACED KICKS

Onitsuka Tiger and Tokyo's Mita Sneakers brought us this take on the iconic Fabre BL-L sneaker in 2013.

The Fabre BL-L was based on a classic basketball shoe from 1975 (the name Fabre is derived from the FAstBREak move in basketball) and was characterized by the innovative slit-cut outsole design, which became a registered trademark of Onitsuka Tiger in the 70s; the three long cuts running the length of the outsole help to improve lateral motion.

With a mix of black and white suede and synthetic fur, the design took inspiration from Ri Ri and Shin Shin, two giant pandas living at Ueno Zoo in Tokyo. Mita's signature chain link design could be found on the insoles.

ASICS GEL-LYTE III
'SELVEDGE DENIM' x RONNIE FIEG

CLASSIC AMERICAN DENIM

To mark the first anniversary of his KITH store's opening, it was a natural step for Ronnie Fieg to celebrate in conjunction with ASICS, a brand he holds close to his heart.

Taking inspiration from a room in the KITH flagship SoHo premises – made of bricks from 1950, century-old wood and American steel – the selvedge denim upper represented the durability and toughness of the store and its heritage.

To round out the Americana theme, white leather 'tiger stripes' with a red trim – a colourway that gives a nod to the American flag – was utilized across the upper.

The Selvedge Denim Gel-Lyte IIIs were only available to purchase through KITH locations and its online store.

SHOE DATA

EDITION
'Selvedge Denim'
PACK
'Ronnie Fieg'
YEAR RELEASED
2012
ORIGINAL PURPOSE
Running
TECHNOLOGY
GEL Cushioning System;
split tongue

ASICS GEL-SAGA II
'MAZARINE BLUE' x RONNIE FIEG

THE BUTTERFLY EFFECT

Ronnie Fieg's partnership with ASICS extends
back to his days working at New York retailer
David Z, where he first started at the age of
fifteen; during that time he has produced a
number of memorable collaborations with the
Japanese brand.

Inspired by the colour of the unique mazarine
blue butterfly, the model consists of a nubuck
upper with a perforated toe box and side panels,
with black top eyelets, lining and midsole
adding contrast.

Only 300 pairs were produced, with both KITH
locations having an allocation of ninety pairs each
along with a matching Canadian fleece letterman
varsity jacket. The remaining pairs were distributed
to select ASICS accounts.

SHOE DATA
EDITION
'Mazarine Blue'
PACK
Ronnie Fieg
YEAR RELEASED
2011
ORIGINAL PURPOSE
Running
TECHNOLOGY
GEL Cushioning System

SHOE DATA

EDITION
'Super Red 2.0'
PACK
Ronnie Fieg
YEAR RELEASED
2012
ORIGINAL PURPOSE
Running
TECHNOLOGY
GEL Cushioning System

ASICS GT-II 'SUPER RED 2.0' x RONNIE FIEG

RONNIE FIEG'S SEEING RED

This 2012 edition was an updated version of Ronnie Fieg's 'Super Red' Gel-Lyte III that had been released via New York retailer David Z in 2010.

For this version, Fieg worked on a GT-II that featured the 'Super Red' colourway applied all over the pigskin suede upper, with grey accents surrounding the Tiger stripes and a two-tone grey sole unit.

These were only available through KITH locations and its online store, and they sold out almost instantly.

ASICS GT-II
'OLYMPIC TEAM NETHERLANDS'

GOING DUTCH

At the London 2012 Olympic Games every brand wanted to represent its country, including the Team Netherlands sponsor, ASICS, whose choice of model for the Games was the GT-II. The sneaker was worn by the team at the opening and closing ceremonies and was the official delegation shoe for the Dutch athletes.

Matching the Netherlands' orange strip, the model featured a predominantly orange suede-and-nylon upper, white leather 3M-trimmed stripes, white nylon covering the toe box and synthetic suede on the lace stay and heeltab.

Other features included '2012' on the lace aglets, the colours of the Dutch flag on the sole and two of the top eyelets, gold laces, gold branding on the tongue label and text on the heeltab, and 'Nederland' on the insole.

The sneakers were sold via select ASICS accounts worldwide, with a pre-release a week before at the SEVENTYFIVE store in Amsterdam, at which seventy-five pairs were sold with a special Olympics bag.

SHOE DATA

EDITION
'Olympic Team Netherlands'
YEAR RELEASED
2012
ORIGINAL PURPOSE
Running
TECHNOLOGY
GEL Cushioning System

SHOE DATA
EDITION
'Wildcats'
PACK
'Hanon'
YEAR RELEASED
2011
ORIGINAL PURPOSE
Running
TECHNOLOGY
GEL Cushioning System;
split tongue
EXTRAS
Dust bag

ASICS GEL-LYTE III x HANON 'WILDCATS'

GOOOOOOO WILDCATS!

In 2011 Hanon Shop in Aberdeen teamed up with ASICS to create its own version of the classic Gel-Lyte III model.

Drawing inspiration from a local running club called The Wildcats, Hanon swapped the usual materials for more luxurious choices, using a mustard-yellow and burgundy perforated suede upper alongside a woven collar lining. The Hanon 'Keeps on Burning' logo featured on the 3M tonal stripes, with further dual branding on the tongue label, heel and insole.

The first fifty customers received a bespoke dual-branded shoe bag, while every other pair sold through Hanon came with a dust bag screened with the logo.

The 'Wildcats' were sold exclusively through Hanon in the UK and a few select retailers worldwide.

ASICS GEL-LYTE III
x ALIFE RIVINGTON CLUB

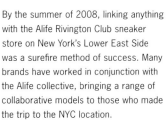

REVELLING IN RIVINGTON

By the summer of 2008, linking anything with the Alife Rivington Club sneaker store on New York's Lower East Side was a surefire method of success. Many brands have worked in conjunction with the Alife collective, bringing a range of collaborative models to those who made the trip to the NYC location.

Released in a twin pack, this sneaker took a mix of colours and detailing and employed them to good effect. The outer heel label was a notch above the printed branding traditionally employed by most collaborators, while the nylon and suede paired on the upper in a curry/white/blue colour combination ensured a premium feel. A charcoal grey version was also released at the same time.

These appeared in the summer of 2008 and sold out instantly in-store and online.

SHOE DATA
EDITION
Alife Rivington Club
YEAR RELEASED
2008
ORIGINAL PURPOSE
Running
TECHNOLOGY
GEL Cushioning System

ASICS GEL-LYTE III
x SLAM JAM
'5TH DIMENSION'

ASICS TO THE 5TH DIMENSION

Milanese boutique Slam Jam reworked ASICS' popular
runner in 2010, applying a mix of mesh fabrics
with the aim of keeping the colours simple and the
textures elaborate.

The shoe showcases light and dark grey that fade
through to a head-turning red with bright blue accents.
A gradient midsole fades from red to white on the outer
and black to white on the medial side.

The '5th Dimension' refers to the theory that there is a
further dimension, or timeline, within which the choices
we make in life will generate different outcomes.

A special pack – including a pair of matching socks,
a drawstring bag and record – was exclusively sold at
Slam Jam, limited to 96 pairs, while the sneakers on
their own were limited to 276 pairs, distributed to select
ASICS retailers worldwide.

SHOE DATA

EDITION
'5th Dimension'
PACK
'Slam Jam'
YEAR RELEASED
2010
ORIGINAL PURPOSE
Running
TECHNOLOGY
GEL Cushioning System;
split tongue
EXTRAS
Extra laces; 7" vinyl record;
drawstring bag; socks

ASICS GT-II x SNS 'SEVENTH SEAL'

CHECKMATE

Following a collaboration with ASICS on the GT-II in 2011, Sneakersnstuff was invited to work on the model again in 2012, and this time approached it with a chessboard theme.

The concept was inspired by the famous Swedish film *The Seventh Seal*, directed by Ingmar Bergman in 1957, which was based around a medieval knight who is seeking answers while playing a game of chess with Death.

The design consisted of a premium black nubuck upper, chess-piece detailing on the insole and heel, a chequered lining, and reversed 3M-based tiger stripes on the lateral and medial of the shoe.

A worldwide release was originally planned, but due to a production fault that caused some chess pieces to come out blue instead of white, only 158 pairs were made available to the public via the Sneakersnstuff store and online.

SHOE DATA

EDITION
'Seventh Seal'
PACK
'SNS'
YEAR RELEASED
2012
ORIGINAL PURPOSE
Running
TECHNOLOGY
GEL Cushioning System

ASICS GT-II **PROPER**

RUNNING LONG BEACH

In 2004 collaborations with footwear brands were a relatively new concept, and the selection of shoes being offered to potential partners was small.

Working with a specialist brand such as ASICS presented an exciting opportunity to footwear boutique PROPER. With ASICS' base so close to the PROPER store in Long Beach, California, the connection between the two companies was authentic.

The classic GT-II runner was a clever choice for the collaboration; it has a slimmed-down silhouette with various panels on which to showcase creativity. For this edition dark ripstop sections sat alongside olive-green suede and nylon, with a bright orange accent adding a little extra focus to the opulence, while the ASICS stripes were represented in black.

Only 150 pairs of the GT-II PROPER were released, available exclusively from the Long Beach store.

SHOE DATA
EDITION
PROPER
YEAR RELEASED
2004
ORIGINAL PURPOSE
Running
TECHNOLOGY
GEL Cushioning System

SHOE DATA

EDITION
Footpatrol
YEAR RELEASED
2012
ORIGINAL
Running
TECHNOLOGY
GEL Cushioning System
EXTRAS
Extra laces;
dust bag; wooden box

ASICS GEL-SAGA II x FOOTPATROL

A LONDON SAGA

For this 2012 reworking of the Gel-Saga II, ASICS joined forces with London-based sneaker store Footpatrol.

The inspiration came from Footpatrol's store interior, as well as natural materials such as wood and rubber. The shoe has an asymmetrical design, with the logo stripes on the lateral side featuring 3M reflective materials, while further asymmetric detailing could be seen on the heel counter and sockliner. The rich suede camel-coloured upper was offset with blue accents.

The Gel-Saga II initially went on sale exclusively at Footpatrol's Soho store and came with two sets of additional laces and a limited edition dust bag. The first 100 customers who bought the shoe also received a numbered wooden shoebox. Following the store release, the Gel-Saga II shipped globally a week later.

FIRST OF MANY FOR PATTA

For its first collaboration with ASICS, Dutch sneaker store Patta wanted to make the shoe as memorable as possible.

Drawing inspiration from the red, white and black coat of arms of the city of Amsterdam, Patta used these colours on various panels alongside its own Patta green. Crosses from the coat of arms featured on the leather lining, mismatched insoles and a speckled sole unit. Leather, perforated leather, suede and 3M could all be found across the upper.

Each of the 250 pairs came with a matching backpack. A capsule collection of T-shirts, caps and a varsity jacket were also produced to commemorate the collaboration.

SHOE DATA
EDITION
Patta
YEAR RELEASED
2007
ORIGINAL PURPOSE
Running
TECHNOLOGY
GEL Cushioning System
EXTRAS
Backpack

ASICS GEL-LYTE III x PATTA

CONVERSE

Converse's ubiquitous Chuck Taylor silhouette, one of the most recognizable shoe designs in the world today, has consistently been adopted by a range of subcultures. From its long-running associations with music, street fashion and urban culture, it is a shoe that has become a staple of everyday life for many people around the globe.

Beyond the now-classic Chuck Taylor, the Converse archive contains a range of other models that have been hugely influential and have established yet more defining moments in sneaker culture. The Pro Leather and One Star were serious silhouettes that commanded attention when they were released, and are still high on many wish lists today.

The broad upper of the Chuck Taylor – and the overall simplicity of Converse models in general – provides an ideal canvas for collaborations. This is something that Converse has explored to great effect in a number of outstanding ventures, often within the top-tier First String line, which releases high-quality editions in limited numbers.

From Footpatrol in London (page 68), Patta in Amsterdam (page 69) and Mita Sneakers in Tokyo (page 65) – all shops with a vast knowledge of sneakers – there has been an outpouring of Converse interpretations. But it is the foray into high fashion with Italian label Missoni (page 72), and Converse's work with Canadian fleece and fine-cotton purveyors Reigning Champ (page 73), that have really demonstrated the brand's willingness to push in new directions with fresh and unusual partners.

Further initiatives such as the campaign for (Product)Red (page 64) – a charity project donating to AIDS research – demonstrate how brands can realize creative ambition while also promoting social responsibility.

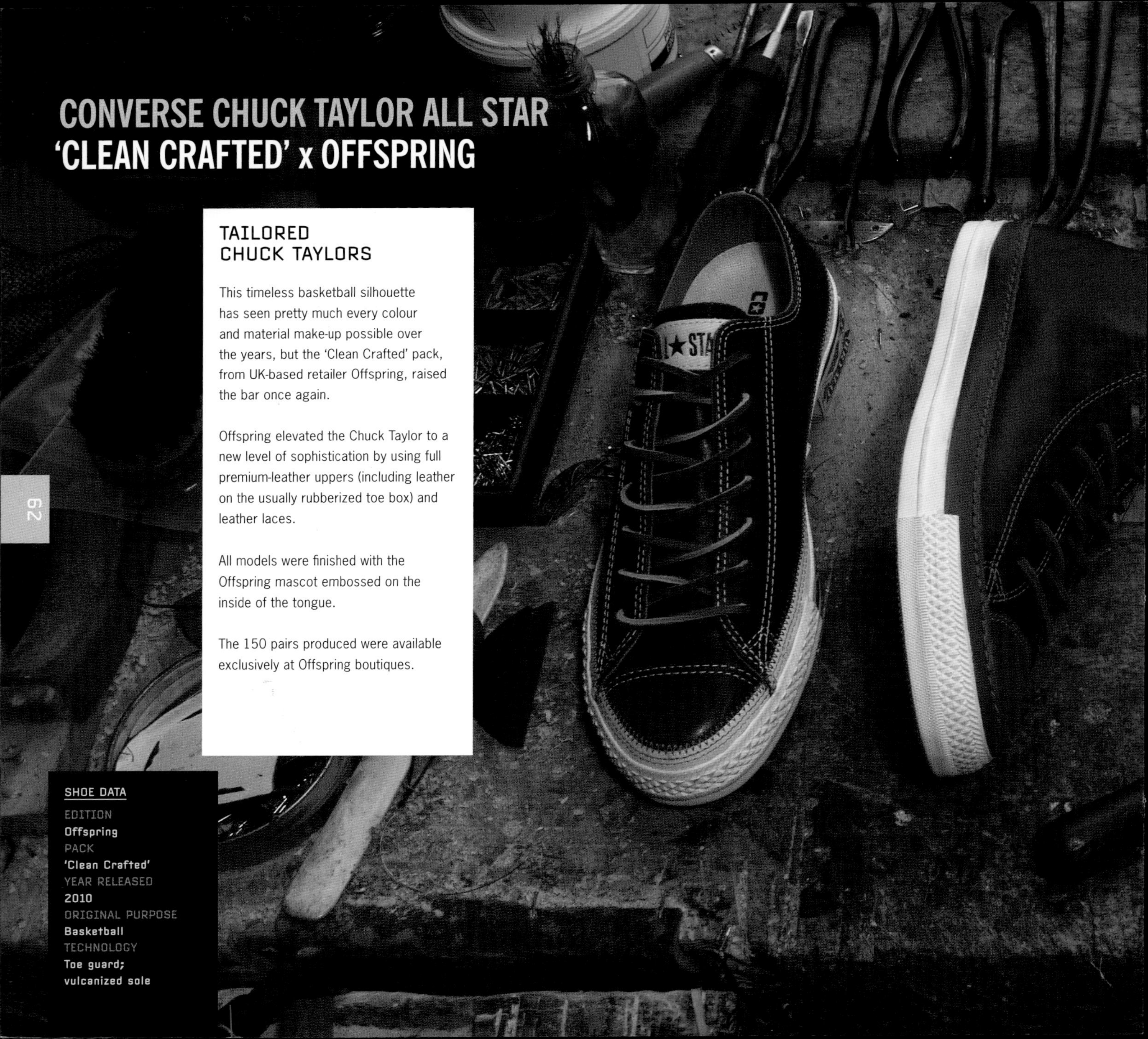

CONVERSE CHUCK TAYLOR ALL STAR
'CLEAN CRAFTED' x OFFSPRING

TAILORED
CHUCK TAYLORS

This timeless basketball silhouette
has seen pretty much every colour
and material make-up possible over
the years, but the 'Clean Crafted' pack,
from UK-based retailer Offspring, raised
the bar once again.

Offspring elevated the Chuck Taylor to a
new level of sophistication by using full
premium-leather uppers (including leather
on the usually rubberized toe box) and
leather laces.

All models were finished with the
Offspring mascot embossed on the
inside of the tongue.

The 150 pairs produced were available
exclusively at Offspring boutiques.

SHOE DATA

EDITION
Offspring
PACK
'Clean Crafted'
YEAR RELEASED
2010
ORIGINAL PURPOSE
Basketball
TECHNOLOGY
**Toe guard;
vulcanized sole**

CONVERSE (PRODUCT)RED
CHUCK TAYLOR ALL STAR HI

SHOE DATA

EDITION
(Product)Red
YEAR RELEASED
2009
ORIGINAL PURPOSE
Basketball
TECHNOLOGY
Toe guard;
vulcanized sole
EXTRAS
Tote bag

CHARITY CASE

Having been around for almost a century, the All Star is a time-honoured and instantly recognizable classic. In 2009 a special edition All Star Hi was made under the (Product)Red initiative, for which brands create unique goods and a percentage of the profit is donated to the The Global Fund to Fight AIDS in Africa.

A motorcycle jacket served as the inspiration for this All Star, with the upper unconventionally split into numerous panels made up entirely of soft red leather, including the toe box.

Heavy-duty zips, snaps and quilted lining reinforced the biker influence.

CONVERSE CHUCK TAYLOR ALL STAR TYO CUSTOM MADE HI x MITA SNEAKERS

CYCLING IN THE RAIN

Tokyo's Mita Sneakers teamed up with Converse for this take on the All Star TYO Custom Made Hi, a contemporary, hi-tech rethinking of the classic Chuck Taylor. The Mita edition featured a water-repellent camouflage upper, further modified with a waterproof side zip in white.

The liner used Thinsulate material for warmth, while a custom sockliner provided added comfort. The Tokyo lifestyle was kept in mind for the design of the toe cap, which was reinforced with a stronger rubber, making it more durable when cycling.

The bold duck-hunting camo design was complemented by metal eyelets and tonal laces, while a chain-link print on the 'Converse Tokyo Custom Made' insole finished off the model.

SHOE DATA

EDITION
Mita Sneakers
YEAR RELEASED
2012
ORIGINAL PURPOSE
Basketball
TECHNOLOGY
Toe guard;
vulcanized sole;
Thinsulate;
bellows

CONVERSE PRO LEATHER MID & OX x BODEGA

BODEGAS TO DIE FOR

Preconceived notions of the Pro Leather were turned upside down when, in 2012, Converse enlisted six concept brands to rework its simple clean-cut lines for the top-tier First String collection. The likes of Stüssy, CLOT, Patta and Boston-based retailer Bodega developed some interesting renditions.

Bodega pushed boundaries with this collaboration, working with some rarely used fabrics and appliqués such as pony hair to give the basketball sneaker a high-fashion edge. The all-over tan colourway with black accents played down the bold upper and accentuated the luxury feel.

The Ox is a flip of the Pro, holding down a black premium-leather upper with faux pony accents. The pack was dubbed 'Ride or Die' and was available at stores with Converse First String accounts.

SHOE DATA

EDITION
First String
PACK
'Bodega "Ride or Die"'
YEAR RELEASED
2012
ORIGINAL PURPOSE
Basketball
TECHNOLOGY
Padded ankle support
EXTRAS
Tote bag;
extra laces

CONVERSE PRO LEATHER MID
x STÜSSY NEW YORK

ALL AMERICANS
JOIN FORCES

When Stüssy was invited to be a part of Converse's Pro Leather project, the US-based streetwear label wanted to portray the classic model as the all-American icon that it is.

This was achieved by drawing inspiration from New York's fashion scene in the 90s – an era with which Stüssy is often associated – and translating this into the upper of the silhouette.

A patchwork of American fabrics included plaid, different shades of denim, corduroy and the Stars and Stripes flag, which was subtly used along the heel strip. The toe box was made up of premium suede. Limited to 125 pairs, these were only sold at the Stüssy New York store.

SHOE DATA

EDITION
First String
PACK
'Stüssy New York'
YEAR RELEASED
2012
ORIGINAL PURPOSE
Basketball
TECHNOLOGY
Padded ankle support
EXTRAS
**Tote bag;
extra laces**

FOOTPATROL
STEP IT UP

The model made famous by NBA legend Julius Erving, aka Dr J, finally got the worldwide recognition it deserved in 2012, when Converse produced a series of the First String Pro Leather Mid and Ox in collaboration with a range of sneaker luminaries.

Footpatrol produced two tonal versions, both featuring premium nubuck uppers with a subtly embroidered Aztec pattern on the tongue, heel strip and innersole. Branding was integrated throughout including a debossed gas mask on the outer heel side of the shoe, embroidered 'FP' on the heeltab, and the bar logo on the innersole of the right foot.

The Mid was limited to 110 pairs and the Ox to 40. To coincide with the release, Footpatrol produced two custom T-shirts – one mint and one grey – with the Aztec print on the chest pocket to match both pairs. The tees were limited to fifty of each colour.

CONVERSE PRO LEATHER
MID & OX x FOOTPATROL

SHOE DATA

EDITION
First String
PACK
'Footpatrol'
YEAR RELEASED
2012
ORIGINAL PURPOSE
Basketball
TECHNOLOGY
Padded ankle support
EXTRAS
Tote bag;
extra laces

PATTA GETS GREEN-FINGERED

The Patta versions of Converse's 2012 First String Pro Leather Mid and Ox models were launched to coincide with the opening of the Dutch sneaker retailer's new store in Zeedijk, Amsterdam.

Taking gardening as inspiration, Patta used earthy tones for both pairs: on the Mid a tonal tan, and on the Ox an olive colourway were applied to the highly durable CORDURA uppers. The military fabric was further brought to life with pops of colour. The Mid was accented with a velour interior in magenta and a deep purple sole; the purple theme continued through the pack, also featuring in the lining of the Ox.

An exclusive Converse x Patta T-shirt was made available in-store only.

SHOE DATA

EDITION
First String
PACK
'Patta'
YEAR RELEASED
2012
ORIGINAL PURPOSE
Basketball
TECHNOLOGY
Padded ankle support
EXTRAS
T-shirt; tote bag;
extra laces

CONVERSE PRO LEATHER & OX x CLOT

EAST MEETS WEST

Hong Kong-based culture collective CLOT held down Converse's First String Pro Leather collaborations in the East in 2012.

For this homage to the Pro Leather, CLOT went with a vintage feel, showcasing the rich heritage of the basketball shoe and its subsequent adoption into fashion and music circles.

Contrary to the name of the model, the upper was made of a stonewashed canvas lined with premium cotton atop an off-white midsole. The colourway was kept in line with the original Pro Leather, with CLOT bringing in its signature red for the branding on the Mid. The low-top Ox utilized the same vintage design aesthetic, with a flip of the Mid's colourway.

Matching red and white T-shirts were also produced to coincide with the release.

The 'First String' collection previewed at CLOT's flagship JUICE store in Hong Kong, followed by a general release in other JUICE Hong Kong, Shanghai, Taipei and Kuala Lumpur stores.

SHOE DATA
EDITION
First String
PACK
'CLOT'
YEAR RELEASED
2012
ORIGINAL PURPOSE
Basketball
TECHNOLOGY
Padded ankle support

ALOHA'S MILITARY SALUTE

This 2012 collaboration was Aloha Rag's second with Converse; the first had celebrated the Hawaii-based high-fashion store's 20th anniversary in 2011. Both were released under Aloha Rag's own label, AR SRPLS, in collections inspired by military basics.

This pack featured a Pro Leather and an Auckland Racer, both of which used a combination of premium leathers and canvases. The Pro Leather showcased a white leather upper with suede accents and a gum sole. Laser-etched stars on the inner side were evocative of army equipment footlockers, while the touch of camouflage print rounded out the theme.

The lightweight and flexible Auckland Racer was influenced by commando-style hiking boots. African goat leather lined fifty per cent of the shoe, providing maximum durability.

CONVERSE PRO LEATHER & AUCKLAND RACER
x ALOHA RAG

SHOE DATA
EDITION
'First String'
PACK
Aloha Rag/AR SRPLS
YEAR RELEASED
2012
ORIGINAL PURPOSE
Basketball; running
TECHNOLOGY
Padded ankle support;
dual-density EVA
midsole; laser

CONVERSE x MISSONI

SHOE DATA

EDITION
Missoni
YEAR RELEASED
2010
ORIGINAL PURPOSE
Basketball; running
TECHNOLOGY
**Toe guard;
vulcanized sole;
rubber sole**

ITALIAN SIGNATURE STYLE

The Converse First String line is dedicated to producing top-tier products for the brand in collaboration with select partners. Past contributors include Kicks Hawaii, sak, Bodega, Reigning Champ and, of course, Missoni.

In 2010 Converse looked to the fashion set. The result was a fusion between Converse's classic silhouettes and the Italian couture house's exquisitely detailed fabrics.

So far, the Missoni collection has included a range of beautifully designed All Star Hi's (below) made up of various signature patterns and materials, as well as a copper-thread knitted Auckland Racer (below left) and a collection of Pro Leather Hi's.

Brand heritage and great craftsmanship go hand in hand, which is why the two brands have worked together so effortlessly over the course of their collaborative relationship.

CONVERSE ALL STAR LO
x REIGNING CHAMP

COTTON CHAMP

While Converse has become iconic through its long association with the world of sport, CYC Design Corp. earned its status through supplying superior-quality cotton garments to the likes of Supreme and Alife. In 2008 it created its own in-house brand, Reigning Champ, with the aim of producing the finest-quality sweats, T-shirts and cotton goods.

Cotton uppers had featured on sneakers before, but none could rival the quality of the heavyweight Canadian terry cotton used on these All Star Lo's.

Further details included the matte black eyelets matching some of the details found on Reigning Champ's garments, natural and matching laces, an Oxford fabric-lined interior, dual-branded detailing on the tongue and insole and the classic Chuck Taylor gum rubber outsole.

SHOE DATA

EDITION
Reigning Champ
YEAR RELEASED
2012
ORIGINAL PURPOSE
Basketball
TECHNOLOGY
Toe guard;
vulcanized scle
EXTRAS
Tote bag

CONVERSE PRO LEATHER
x JORDAN BRAND

30 YEARS OF 23

When freshman Michael Jordan hit the game-winning jump shot in the final seconds of the 1982 NCAA Final for the University of North Carolina (UNC), he was wearing a pair of Converse Pro Leathers.

To commemorate thirty years since the memorable shot, Jordan Brand and Converse joined forces to create this limited edition anniversary pack distributed only via an exclusive online auction.

The pack featured the blue-and-white kit Jordan was wearing on the night, while the size 13 Pro Leathers included a 'UNC 23' basketball design with the iconic 'Jumpman' logo printed on the insoles. Both the University of North Carolina jersey and the Pro Leather sneakers were personally signed by Michael Jordan and came enclosed in a deluxe hardwood box.

Thirty individually numbered packs were commissioned; Jordan kept seven, and twenty-three were made available at auction. All proceeds went to the James R. Jordan Foundation.

SHOE DATA

EDITION
Jordan Brand
PACK
'Limited Edition
Commemorative Pack'
YEAR RELEASED
2012
ORIGINAL PURPOSE
Basketball
TECHNOLOGY
Padded ankle support
EXTRAS
Hardwood box;
basketball jersey;
signed shoes

SHOE DATA

EDITION
Number (N)ine
YEAR RELEASED
2010
ORIGINAL PURPOSE
Basketball
TECHNOLOGY
**Toe guard;
vulcanized sole**

STARS IN THE MAKING

It took an experimental Japanese fashion brand to change the timeless aesthetics of the Converse All Star Ox and One Star Ox. The interpretation of Takahiro Miyashita for Number (N)ine recalled his favourite childhood Converse model, the Odessa. Number (N)ine integrated the Odessa's asymmetrical lacing with a premium deerskin suede upper. Original features of both the One Star and the All Star were apparent in the panelling and silver eyelets of Miyashita's All Star Ox (shown here in yellow). Each interpretation also featured a metallic star on the side of the heel: gold for the All Star and silver for the One Star.

CONVERSE ASYMMETRICAL
ALL STAR OX & ONE STAR OX x NUMBER (N)INE

NEW BALANCE

From a humble beginning as the New Balance Arch Company, an orthopaedic shoemaker specializing in arch supports and remedial footwear, New Balance has grown to become an iconic athletic footwear company with manufacturing bases in both the United States and the United Kingdom, a rarity in today's increasingly Asia-centric manufacturing supply chain. Its 'Made in UK' and 'Made in the USA' ranges are both recognized as hallmarks of quality and excellence in craftsmanship.

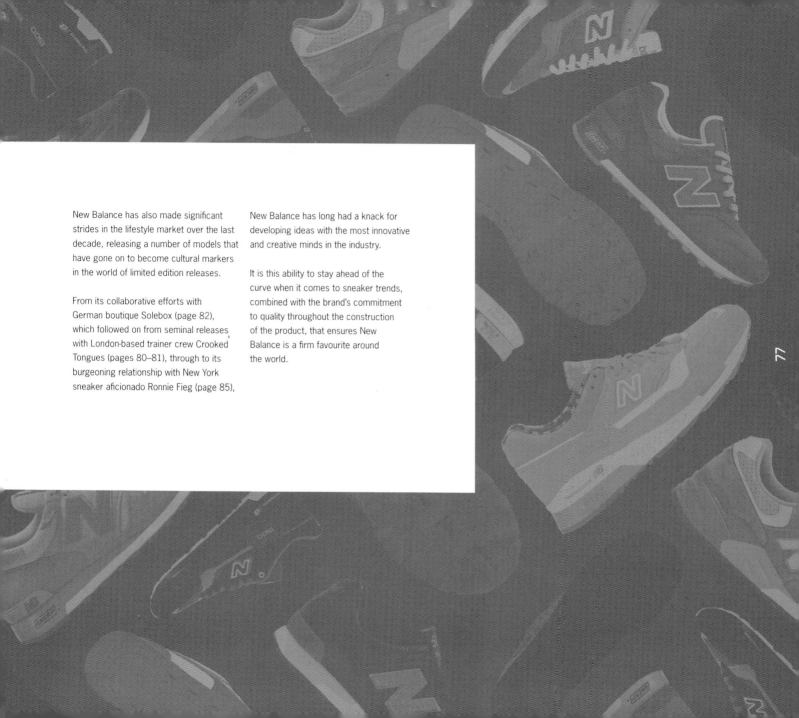

New Balance has also made significant strides in the lifestyle market over the last decade, releasing a number of models that have gone on to become cultural markers in the world of limited edition releases.

From its collaborative efforts with German boutique Solebox (page 82), which followed on from seminal releases with London-based trainer crew Crooked Tongues (pages 80–81), through to its burgeoning relationship with New York sneaker aficionado Ronnie Fieg (page 85),

New Balance has long had a knack for developing ideas with the most innovative and creative minds in the industry.

It is this ability to stay ahead of the curve when it comes to sneaker trends, combined with the brand's commitment to quality throughout the construction of the product, that ensures New Balance is a firm favourite around the world.

NEW BALANCE x OFFSPRING

NOT JUST FUNCTIONAL

New Balance's 'Made in UK' division has always maintained solid relationships with sports retailers, but it was London-based Offspring that became one of its first fashion accounts, and helped to propel the brand into the consciousness of style connoisseurs.

After twelve months of seeding product, the brands decided to cement the burgeoning relationship by celebrating Offspring's four London stores with the first New Balance 'Made in UK' dual-branded collaboration.

The sneakers were made in the New Balance factory in Flimby. Each of Offspring's stores was represented in the designs, and had their individual store numbers stitched onto the heel. The final result was a pack of four sneakers inspired by an autumnal colour palette.

SHOE DATA

EDITION
Offspring
YEAR RELEASED
2006
ORIGINAL PURPOSE
Running
TECHNOLOGY
C-Cap

EDITION
**Crooked Tongues
'Black Sword'**
PACK
'Confederation of Villainy'
YEAR RELEASED
2006
ORIGINAL PURPOSE
Running
TECHNOLOGY
ENCAP
EXTRAS
**Custom double box;
extra laces**

NEW BALANCE M577 'BLACK SWORD'
x CROOKED TONGUES & BJ BETTS

CHINESE GANGSTER GETS INKED

Representing the nationalities of four Crooked Tongues crew members, each model within the New Balance 'Confederation of Villainy' pack portrays a notorious villain who came from the member's hometown.

The pack's M577 execution was named 'Black Sword' and represented Song Jiang, the leader of a gang of Chinese outlaws who lived in Shanghai during the Song Dynasty.

Each shoe in the pack featured a white top eyelet, premium materials and a pop colour.

Custom boxes accompanied each release, featuring unique work by tattoo artist BJ Betts that personified the villains. Individual models were limited to 99 pairs, only sold through the Crooked Tongues online store.

NEW BALANCE M1500 'BLACKBEARD'
x CROOKED TONGUES & BJ BETTS

A RUNNER WITH A DARK STORY

The New Balance and Crooked Tongues 'Confederation of Villainy' pack featured the M1500, which had often been the subject of collaborations, so the CT crew paid extra attention to detail to ensure that the execution was memorable.

Blackbeard was the English pirate chosen to represent the city of Bristol. He allegedly wore lit matches woven into his beard, and so a dark colourway of black, grey and white was chosen, with a splash of red throughout. Using a mix of leather and mesh on the upper kept the textures varied, while contrast stitching added a premium touch.

SHOE DATA

EDITION
Crooked Tongues 'Blackbeard'
PACK
'Confederation of Villainy'
YEAR RELEASED
2006
ORIGINAL PURPOSE
Running
TECHNOLOGY
ENCAP
EXTRAS
**Custom double box;
x2 laces**

NEW BALANCE M1500
x CROOKED TONGUES
x SOLEBOX

BREAD & BUTTER
BRAND SANDWICH

The year 2005 marked the first Bread & Butter street fashion trade show in Berlin, at which brands showcase their upcoming collections. During the event, the Crooked Tongues and Solebox teams released their very limited and exclusive collaboration in conjunction with New Balance.

Designed by Chris Law of Crooked Tongues with Hikmet from Solebox, the shoe was inspired by the colour palette of the old Crooked Tongues website.

Only fifty pairs were produced; each came with an individually numbered hang tag that displayed 'CT-SB' in embossed lettering.

SHOE DATA

EDITION
Crooked Tongues
x Solebox
YEAR RELEASED
2005
ORIGINAL PURPOSE
Running
TECHNOLOGY
ENCAP
EXTRAS
Individually numbered
hang tag

SHOE DATA
EDITION
Solebox
PACK
Purple Devils
YEAR RELEASED
2006
ORIGINAL PURPOSE
Running
EXTRAS
ENCAP, C-Cap

NEW BALANCE x SOLEBOX 'PURPLE DEVILS'

THE DEVIL IS IN THE DETAILS

In 2006 the Solebox team released a pack consisting of three sneakers: a 'Made in UK' 575, a 576 and a 1500 (1500 and 576 are pictured here) that were known as the 'Purple Devils'.

Each model featured a predominantly black suede and premium-leather upper, 3M accents, purple suede front panels and a classic white midsole with contrasting gum sole unit. The shoes also featured a branded Solebox lace jewel.

All three were given an extremely limited release: the 575 was first, with a run of 120 pairs worldwide; the 576 and 1500 saw a production run of only 300 pairs of each model.

NEW BALANCE M576
x FOOTPATROL

A STICKY SITUATION

For its 'Made in UK' New Balance M576, Footpatrol came up with a design reminiscent of late-90s skate shoes that featured swappable Velcro logos.

The application of various neon colours against a premium-leather upper ensured the release was unique; the wearer could alternate the various coloured 'N's and laces supplied with the shoe.

Available in both black and brown, the release also included a specially embroidered Footpatrol-branded gas mask hang tag that could be stuck firmly to its side.

The idea proved popular and New Balance later released further models in line with this concept.

SHOE DATA

EDITION
Footpatrol
YEAR RELEASED
2007
ORIGINAL PURPOSE
Running
TECHNOLOGY
C-Cap
EXTRAS
Extra laces; interchangeable Velcro 'N' logo and Footpatrol logo

NEW BALANCE ML999 'STEEL BLUE' x RONNIE FIEG
& NEW BALANCE M1300 'SALMON SOLE' x RONNIE FIEG

STEEL BLUE IS THE LOOK

New York designer Ronnie Fieg and his store KITH have consistently produced well-executed sneaker make-ups, and the two New Balance models shown here are no exception.

Fieg's 'Steel Blue' collection from 2012 provided a range of highlights, including these 'Made in USA' ML999s (below right). Details included New Balance branding debossed on the heel and tongue, 'Just Us' written on the lace aglets and the KITH logo imprinted on the insoles.

To mark the special release, 100 handmade wooden boxes containing the sneakers, hoodie and sweat shorts were made available at KITH Manhattan and Brooklyn stores. Regular boxed versions were sold via select New Balance stockists worldwide.

Using a similar theme to his Salmon Toe ASICS Gel-Lyte III from 2011, Ronnie then reinforced his collaborative flair on the classic New Balance M1300 model (above right). An exclusive matching 'Made in USA' varsity jacket from Shades of Grey by Micah Cohen was also made available at both store locations.

SHOE DATA

EDITION
KITH/Ronnie Fieg
YEAR RELEASED
2012
ORIGINAL PURPOSE
Running
TECHNOLOGY
ENCAP

SHOE DATA

EDITION
KITH/Ronnie Fieg
YEAR RELEASED
2012
ORIGINAL PURPOSE
Running
TECHNOLOGY
ABZORB
EXTRAS
Extra laces; hang tag; wooden box; hoodie; sweat shorts

SHOE DATA

EDITION
Hanon
PACK
'Northern Sole'
YEAR RELEASED
2012
ORIGINAL PURPOSE
Running
TECHNOLOGY
ENCAP
EXTRAS
Wooden box;
dust bag

NORTHERN EXPOSURE

Aberdeen's Hanon Shop added to its 'Northern Sole' New Balance collection with the release of this M1500, entitled 'Chosen Few'.

Drawing on New Balance's 'Made in UK' heritage models for inspiration, Hanon used various signature materials, such as the navy European suede found on the original classic M577 and M576, to construct the silhouette.

The design also featured Wolverine suede pigskin on the upper, which had been tanned to be both stain- and fade-resistant. Awash with greys and blues, it created a look that was reminiscent of models featured in vintage sneaker catalogues.

The initial drop was in the Hanon store, with the first fifty customers receiving a limited edition wooden box. An online release of a small quantity followed the next day.

NEW BALANCE M1500 'CHOSEN FEW' x HANON

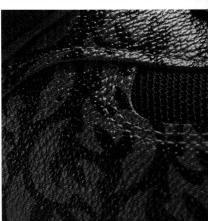

SHOE DATA

EDITION
House 33 x
Crooked Tongues
YEAR RELEASED
2005
ORIGINAL PURPOSE
Running
TECHNOLOGY
C-Cap

NEW BALANCE M576
x HOUSE 33
x CROOKED TONGUES

THE ONE AND ONLY

Back in 2005 Crooked Tongues had close affiliations with prolific type foundry and clothing label House 33. While they were neighbours in London's Soho, they developed close ties with House Industries founder Andy Cruz and tattoo artist BJ Betts, a long-time House contributor.

When Crooked Tongues had the opportunity to visit New Balance's 'Made in UK' factory, based in Flimby, Cumbria, they took with them specially made Italian full-grain premium leather emblazoned with the House 33 motif. From there, they created this unique one-off pair of New Balance M576s. Earmarked with 'C.T.' on the tongue of the right foot, 'H.33.' on the left, and complemented by distinguished mesh panelling, these truly are one of a kind.

SHOE DATA

EDITION
realmadHECTIC x
Mita Sneakers
PACK
'10th Anniversary'
YEAR RELEASED
2010
ORIGINAL PURPOSE
Running
TECHNOLOGY
Rollbar

NEW BALANCE MT580 '10TH ANNIVERSARY' x REALMADHECTIC x MITA SNEAKERS

A DECADE OF GREAT DESIGN

In 2010 Japanese brand realmadHECTIC celebrated its 10th anniversary with a series of New Balance sneakers produced in collaboration with fellow Tokyo residents Mita Sneakers.

The MT580 'BKX' featured a black quilted-leather upper on top of a faux-woodgrain midsole, finished off with standard white at the front and an interesting toe cap structure.

Just like the preceding offerings in the 10th anniversary series, the insole featured an all-over print of all the previous MT580 releases.

NEW BALANCE M1500 x LA MJC x COLETTE

'VIVRE SANS TEMPS MORT'

Since starting up in 2001, French communications agency La MJC has become a well-known name within street culture and sneaker communities. It has worked on multiple sneaker collaborations with brands including New Balance, Nike, ASICS, Sebago, Lacoste and Supra, not to mention its ongoing series of *All Gone* books.

This collaboration with Paris über-boutique Colette sported the motto 'Vivre sans temps mort', which roughly translates as 'Live like there's no tomorrow', printed onto the insoles.

The use of pigskin suede and premium leather on the upper positioned the sneakers as a luxury item while the red/white/grey colour blocking and subtle touch of 3M perfectly complemented the silhouette. The shoes also came with three pairs of laces: white, grey and red, matching each colour used on the upper.

SHOE DATA

EDITION
La MJC x Colette
YEAR RELEASED
2010
ORIGINAL PURPOSE
Running
TECHNOLOGY
ENCAP
EXTRAS
x3 extra laces

NEW BALANCE MT580 x REALMADHECTIC

LUCKY EIGHTS

New Balance and realmadHECTIC
have enjoyed an ongoing relationship,
producing many successful collaborations
that have pushed the boundaries of
colourway and fabric make-ups.

A favourite HECTIC model is the MT580,
the trail running version of the New
Balance 580, which had an oversized
Rollbar system in the sole unit to prevent
the foot from pronating.

This version was known as the 'Eighth
Bullet' as it was the eighth sneaker to
come from the partnership. A pack of
two designs was released, both of
which featured an interesting mix of
nylon and nubuck – the version shown
here has a navy base colour complete
with pop accents.

SHOE DATA

EDITION
realmadHECTIC
YEAR RELEASED
2005
ORIGINAL PURPOSE
Trail running
TECHNOLOGY
Rollbar

NEW BALANCE CM1700
x WHIZ LIMITED
x MITA SNEAKERS

SHOE DATA

EDITION
**WHIZ LIMITED x
Mita Sneakers**
YEAR RELEASED
2012
ORIGINAL PURPOSE
Running
TECHNOLOGY
**ABZORB;
ENCAP;
C-Cap; laser**

STAR QUALITY

In 2012 New Balance, in conjunction with Japanese powerhouses WHIZ LIMITED and Mita Sneakers, brought us another stellar collaborative release with this take on the New Balance CM1700.

The ventilation holes were updated by laser-cutting them into star shapes and adding a glow-in-dark underlay to make them shine. The upper wore two different colours – red on the medial and navy blue on the lateral – while touches of silver and off-white contrasted with the tricolour blocking. Unique triple branding was also featured on the sockliner.

SHOE DATA

EDITION
Paris Saint-Germain
PACK
'La MJC x Colette
x Undefeated'
YEAR RELEASED
2012
ORIGINAL PURPOSE
Running
TECHNOLOGY
Rollbar

SHOE DATA

EDITION
UCLA Bruins
PACK
'La MJC x Colette
x Undefeated'
YEAR RELEASED
2012
ORIGINAL PURPOSE
Running
TECHNOLOGY
ENCAP

NEW BALANCE CM1500 & MT580
x LA MJC x COLETTE x UNDEFEATED

REPRESENTING THEIR HOMETOWN BALLERS

In 2012 New Balance teamed up with long-time partners La MJC, Parisian boutique Colette and Californian streetwear giants Undefeated to create a CM1500 and an MT580.

Each drew inspiration from the brands' home towns. The CM1500 was influenced by Undefeated's Californian heritage, displaying the UCLA Bruins' yellow/blue colourway, while the MT580 took influence from the Paris Saint-Germain football strip. Both versions featured intricate detailing and materials, all the way down to the sockliner. The CM1500 interior was inspired by the animal kingdom, with leopard lining on the branded insole. The MT580 was subtler, with a French terry material covering the New Balance branding on the sides and Paris Saint-Germain's tricoloured stripes on the insole.

NEW BALANCE M1500 'TOOTHPASTE' x SOLEBOX

SHOE DATA
EDITION
Solebox
PACK
'Toothpaste'
YEAR RELEASED
2007
ORIGINAL PURPOSE
Running
TECHNOLOGY
ENCAP
EXTRAS
Toothbrush; tote bag

SO FRESH, SO CLEAN

The 'Toothpaste' pack from Berlin boutique Solebox featured mint and orange suede accents against pearly-patent white leather, with the bonus inclusion of a gum sole. The double drop also included a toothbrush for each of the two colours, as well as a bespoke tote bag in which to store the sneakers.

Details on each M1500 included a combination patent-leather, suede and mesh upper with the familiar 'Made in England' branding on the tongue, a leather foot bed stamped with a 'Selected Edition' call out, and two subtle metal buttons at the top of the eyelets, one with 'Solebox' etched into it and the other with that pair's individual number out of 216 (the total quantity produced).

A few pairs made for family and friends also had the Solebox logo debossed on the side.

NEW BALANCE M577 x SNS x MILKCRATE

FROM STOCKHOLM TO BALTIMORE

For their fifth collaboration with New Balance, the Stockholm sneaker aficionados and retail maestros at Sneakersnstuff (SNS) brought Baltimore-born DJ, producer, clothing designer and Milkcrate Athletics head honcho Aaron LaCrate into the mix to design one of the two M577s in this pack.

SNS kept it subtle, using tonal grey suede and white perforated leather, while Aaron LaCrate looked to the vibrant colours used in his Milkcrate Athletics clothing line, with a mix of pink, yellow, green and purple suede on the upper, 3M detailing on the tongue and the same

white perforated leather on the toe box and upper panel. Other features included a dual-branded swing tag.

These shoes were only available through top-tier New Balance stockists worldwide.

SHOE DATA
EDITION
SNS x Milkcrate
YEAR RELEASED
2012
ORIGINAL PURPOSE
Running
TECHNOLOGY
ENCAP
EXTRAS
Stickers

94

NIKE

From its origin in 1964 as Blue Ribbon Sports, product-testing new sports footwear ideas through the University of Oregon track team, to its modern-day standing as one of the world's best-known brands, the importance of Nike on the culture and business of athletic footwear can never be overestimated. Nike has long surpassed its original purpose as an athletic footwear company to become a global institution with far-reaching influence in the fields of fashion, music, sport and popular culture.

The names of iconic Nike designers such as Bill Bowerman, Phil Knight and Tinker Hatfield have become ingrained in the consciousness of sneaker enthusiasts around the world. And the company was one of the first to recognize the value of restricting the distribution of certain models, following the basic economics of supply and demand, which has led to the culture of limited edition releases that generate buzz in the sneaker world today.

Nike was also one of the first to introduce the idea of limited edition colourways; basketball models in college-specific colour make-ups were only available to college team players, and went on to become highly collectable in their own right.

From a design perspective, Nike has produced some of the world's definitive sneakers. Seminal early basketball models such as the Air Force 1 and Dunk ignited both the courts and the streets. The Air Max 1 redefined the running shoe in 1987, and continued to do so in 1990 and 1995, with further game-changing releases in footwear design.

Nike has consistently been ahead of the curve in conceptualizing and producing innovative, in-demand shoes. No brand has embraced the business of limited edition releases and third-party collaborative efforts like Nike has. Within Hyperstrike, Nike's top-tier range, designs are usually limited to under fifty pairs and distributed only among friends and family. The slightly less exclusive Tier Zero account initiative was the first to limit physical distribution of a product to select retailers. The next level down, Quickstrike, releases models in larger numbers, to more high-end stores on the high street. Some Quickstrike and Hyperstrike editions have gone on to be viewed as pivotal in the history of athletic footwear.

This preoccupation with innovation through collaboration realized its full potential in the HTM collective, the result of an ongoing collaboration between Fragment Design head honcho Hiroshi Fujiwara, Nike designer Tinker Hatfield and Nike CEO Mark Parker. HTM has been responsible for an incredible array of footwear over the years, including the Flyknit collection (pages 152–53), which was one of the sneaker highlights of 2012. Nike continues to advance footwear design through the application of new technologies and the combination of earlier archive models to create new hybrids.

Third-party collaborators have always been keen to work with the Beaverton behemoth – some of the greatest moments in recent Nike history are the result of creative partnerships, from Patta's interpretation of the Air Max 1 (pages 116–17), to hip-hop impresario Kanye West's design for his very own silhouette, the Air Yeezy (page 154). Nike is not afraid to take bold steps when it comes to limited edition footwear and the culture that surrounds it.

NIKE CORTEZ PREMIUM
x MARK SMITH
& TOM LUEDECKE

NEW TECHNOLOGY FOR SCORCHING PATTERNS

In the world of sneakers, lasers have mainly been used to precision-cut pattern pieces, but in 2003 designer Mark Smith from Nike's Innovation Kitchen introduced a new laser technique that is still in use today.

Smith and fellow Nike designer Tom Luedecke each produced a Premium Cortez inspired by Celtic and tribal artwork, using a laser to etch the pattern into the upper.

This innovation worked best on a large canvas space, which motivated Mark to create a one-piece upper for the Cortez, reducing the panelling and overall weight of the sneaker.

SHOE DATA
EDITION
Mark Smith & Tom Luedecke
PACK
'2003 Laser Project'
YEAR RELEASED
2003
ORIGINAL PURPOSE
Running
TECHNOLOGY
One-piece upper;
herringbone sole; laser
EXTRAS
Slide-out box; cloth wrapping;
numbered leather hang tag

EDITION
Halle Berry
PACK
'Artist Series'
YEAR RELEASED
2004
ORIGINAL PURPOSE
Running
TECHNOLOGY
Air
EXTRAS
Slide-out box; rift socks;
Artist Series hang tag

NIKE AIR RIFT
x HALLE BERRY

HALLE-LUJAH

For its Artist Series, Nike combined the influence and talents of A-list celebrities to give back to those in need. The third set in the series featured actress Halle Berry's take on the Air Rift. An interesting combination of bluish greys and oranges was applied to suede and synthetics. Only 1,050 were made, each individually numbered.

The Rifts came with matching split-toe socks and were housed in a special box. All profits were donated to Berry's chosen charity, the Make-A-Wish Foundation for children with life-threatening conditions.

NIKE AIR HUARACHE
'ACG MOWABB PACK'

ALL IN THE GENES: A NIKE FAMILY AFFAIR

The Nike Air Huarache and Nike Air Mowabb have close family ties; they are connected not only by their birth year (1991), but also by their DNA. Both feature the revolutionary 'Huarache' sock fit that was developed by Nike luminary Tinker Hatfield.

The Air Mowabb took on its neoprene sock trait from the Air Huarache, so it then seemed a natural exchange for the Air Huarache to borrow the Mowabb's most acclaimed feature: its ACG (All Conditions Gear) colourways.

The set of three original Mowabb-inspired colour combinations was applied to premium leather. The shoes were sold exclusively in Europe at outlets that held Nike Quickstrike accounts.

SHOE DATA

EDITION
Quickstrike – Europe only
PACK
'ACG Mowabb Pack'
YEAR RELEASED
2007
ORIGINAL PURPOSE
Running
TECHNOLOGY
Air; Huarache
EXTRAS
x2 extra laces

NIKE AIR HUARACHE LIGHT x STÜSSY

DUAL BRANDING FIRST FOR NIKE

The Air Huarache Light first saw a reissue in 2002; a year later Nike followed up with a highly popular brace of the running classic in collaboration with Stüssy.

Available in two versions – acid green/black, and orange/grey – the release proved hugely popular. Along with the avant-garde colourways there was further differentiation from earlier models in the form of leather mudguards. A friends

and family version was also produced in extremely limited numbers, with a Stüssy logo embroidered on the outer side panel, the first time Nike ever featured another brand name on any of its shoes.

SHOE DATA

EDITION
Stüssy
YEAR RELEASED
2003
ORIGINAL PURPOSE
Running
TECHNOLOGY
Air; Huarache;
ghillie lacing

NIKE FREE 5.0 PREMIUM & FREE 5.0 TRAIL x ATMOS

REPTILIAN ROLL CALL

Back in 2006 Nike's Free technology really came in to its own. Among the first to join forces with Nike on the Free 5.0 was long-time collaborative partner Atmos of Tokyo.

Atmos' not-for-the-faint-hearted take on the Nike Free 5.0 Trail gave it a premium treatment, using reflective 3M uppers overlaid with a reptile-skin effect atop the lightweight Free running sole unit.

For the Premium, a double snakeskin effect was applied to a black upper with silver detailing. The hot pink trim and 3M accents really set the shoe off and ensured its desirability.

SHOE DATA

EDITION
Atmos
YEAR RELEASED
2006
ORIGINAL PURPOSE
Running
TECHNOLOGY
Free; ghillie lacing

NIKE AIR FLOW
x SELFRIDGES

SELFRIDGES' TONED-DOWN COMEBACK

The much-anticipated re-release of the Air Flow in 2011 had many fans of the model excited, especially when images of new editions featuring two original colourways surfaced online.

Around the same time, Selfridges gained the rights to sell two colourways of its own Tier Zero Air Flow exclusively within its store on Oxford Street, London.

The Selfridges Air Flow featured the same fabrics as its predecessor, but diverged from the original standout neon colourway, being covered in an all-over tonal black or olive.

With only twenty-four pairs available in each colourway, the shoes sold out instantly on the day of their release.

SHOE DATA

EDITION
Tier Zero
PACK
'Selfridges Tonal'
YEAR RELEASED
2011
ORIGINAL PURPOSE
Running
TECHNOLOGY
Air; Phylon

THE ELEMENTALS

The Air Presto arrived in 2000 to wide acclaim, and the new model was quickly made available in a variety of colours and make-ups.

This never-released promotional pack of four Prestos from 2001/2002 was based on the concept of the four elements – earth, air, fire and water – and featured a never-before-seen padded velour upper. The pack was accompanied by velour-bound books and dust bags.

Each pair was individually numbered out of 328 and had its element name written across the heel counter in place of 'Air' under the Swoosh.

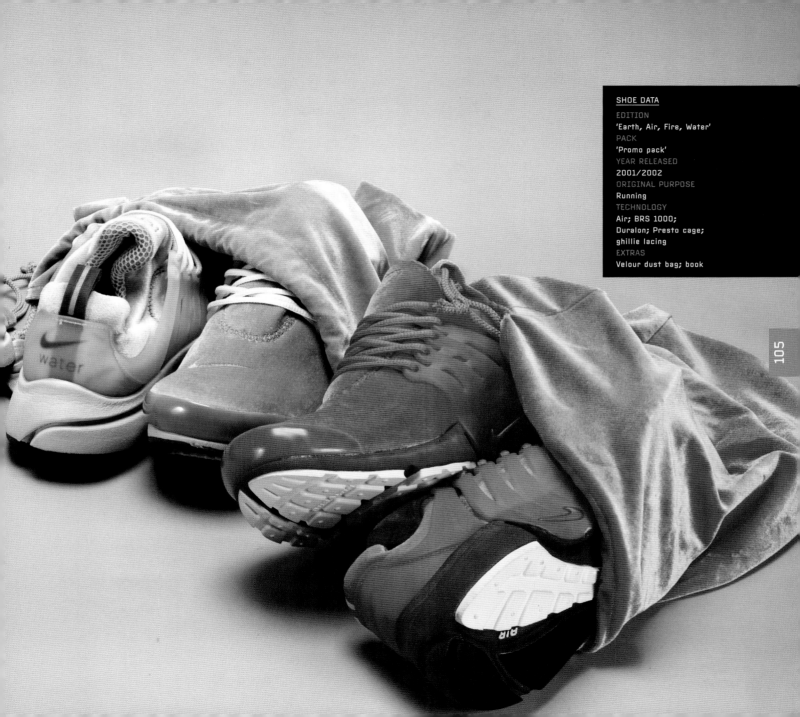

105

NIKE AIR PRESTO
x HELLO KITTY

KAWAII KITTY
FOR THE LADIES

The Air Presto enjoyed a moment in the spotlight when it initially dropped at the turn of the millennium. Widely lauded as 'the T-shirt for your feet', it was presented in a wide range of colours that made it hard to ignore.

When Hello Kitty celebrated its 30th anniversary in 2004, a few major brands were invited to share in the occasion.

For Nike it was the perfect opportunity to combine cute Kitties with the women's Air Presto. A multiple 'cat head' pattern was applied all over the upper, and a pink-and-white version was also created that featured different versions of the Hello Kitty doll. Neither of these was ever made available to the public; just 100 pairs were produced of each, and these were exclusively distributed to friends and family.

SHOE DATA
EDITION
Hello Kitty
PACK
'30th Anniversary'
YEAR RELEASED
2004
ORIGINAL PURPOSE
Running
TECHNOLOGY
Air; BRS 1000;
Duralon; Presto cage;
ghillie lacing

SHOE DATA
EDITION
Sole Collector
(Honolulu NikeTown
exclusive)
YEAR RELEASED
2005
ORIGINAL PURPOSE
Running
TECHNOLOGY
Air; BRS 1000;
Duralon; Presto cage;
ghillie lacing

NIKE AIR PRESTO
'HAWAII EDITION'
x SOLE COLLECTOR

SOLE COLLECTOR PAYS
WORTHY HOMAGE TO
THE 50TH STATE

When *Sole Collector* magazine put together its first set of collaborative models for NikeTown, it made sure that 'The Big Island' wasn't left out of the proceedings.

This Hawaiian hyperstrike edition of the Air Presto was exclusively launched at NikeTown, Honolulu, in an extremely limited offering of only forty-eight pairs.

NIKE AIR PRESTO ROAM x **HTM**

FREE TO ROAM

There have been many variations on the Presto since its first release in 2000, from Clips to Zips and Cages to Roams.

The Air Presto Roam was originally styled as a tougher, more durable Presto. An upgrade to a mid-cut, while keeping the stretch sock-like fit with a padded-out suede upper, meant this version offered more comfort, protection and warmth than its predecessor. Support was preserved with the Presto's customary cage, while a robust sole was made up of Duralon, Nike's blown rubber outsole, which acted much like a foam pad and provided one of the most comfortable rides Nike could offer. To offset Duralon's lack of durability, it was paired with BRS 1000, a highly durable carbon rubber.

The HTM collective worked their magic on these Presto alternatives, producing an autumn/winter-friendly execution, branded with the HTM logo and each pair individually numbered.

The Air Presto Roam was never reproduced after 2002 and remains highly prized by sneaker enthusiasts the world over.

SHOE DATA

EDITION
HTM
YEAR RELEASED
2002
ORIGINAL PURPOSE
Running
TECHNOLOGY
Air; BRS 1000; Duralon;
Presto cage; ghillie lacing
EXTRAS
Special HTM box

SHOE DATA

EDITION
Bodega in-store
exclusive
PACK
'Night Cats'
YEAR RELEASED
2011
ORIGINAL PURPOSE
Running
TECHNOLOGY
Air; Woven;
Footscape

108

NIKE AIR FOOTSCAPE WOVEN CHUKKA x BODEGA

BOSTON'S FINEST BRING THE HEAT ON THE IN-STORE EXCLUSIVE TIP

The Footscape silhouette has always polarized opinion and inspired debate. The innovative lacing system and unusually broad front section of the original model resonated with few on its release in 1995, but over the years it has built up a solid following.

The Footscape Woven refined the shape of the original shoe while pushing the boundaries of construction and use of materials.

When Boston superstore Bodega took the shoe to the drawing board for a collaboration in 2011, the result was the wonderful grey low-top and hazelnut edition that was part of the 'Night Cats' collection.

Bodega also presented in-store customers with this super-limited chukka version, which added a top-tier element to the proceedings.

NIKE AIR
FOOTSCAPE WOVEN
x THE HIDEOUT

FURRY RODENTS BURROW INTO SNEAKER COLLECTIONS

In 2006 the head-turning Footscape silhouette of 1995 was infused with the Nike Woven technique. Several different interpretations saw the light of day, the most memorable of which was the avant-garde execution by London streetwear boutique The Hideout.

Famously called the 'Hamsters' by forum users due to their hairy exterior, these shoes became an instant cult classic and remain highly collectable today.

Designers from The Hideout who worked on the silhouette wanted to portray the shop's Wild West-inspired brand image, and achieved this with a striking premium cowhide and pony-hair upper.

The Hideout version was available in two colourways, grey and brown, which both sold out instantly on their September release.

SHOE DATA

EDITION
Tier Zero
PACK
'The Hideout'
YEAR RELEASED
2006
ORIGINAL PURPOSE
Running
TECHNOLOGY
Air; Woven; Footscape

NIKE AIR WOVEN 'RAINBOW' x HTM

UNIQUE DIP-DYED COLOUR-UPS

Nike's Woven range grabbed the interest of three of the world's biggest sneaker influencers: streetwear designer Hiroshi Fujiwara; Tinker Hatfield, one of Nike's chief designers; and Nike CEO Mark Parker, who collectively formed HTM.

In 2002, two years after the Woven's initial release, HTM carefully chose colours to produce a unique selection of 'Rainbow' Wovens, each taking on a different set of tones in dip-dyed stretch nylon. No two shoes were the same.

As stated on the inner tag, each colourway was limited to 1,500 pairs.

SHOE DATA

EDITION
Tier Zero
PACK
'HTM'
YEAR RELEASED
2002
ORIGINAL PURPOSE
Lifestyle
TECHNOLOGY
Woven; Air;
Phylon midsole

NIKE LUNAR CHUKKA WOVEN **TIER ZERO**

NIKE KEEPS UP THE PACE

In 2002 HTM introduced the Air Woven Chukka Boot. This popular shape was later updated with a Footscape sole and in 2010 Nike's new Lunarlon technology was also integrated into the silhouette.

This interesting fusion of Lunarlon sole and Nike+ technology made this a lifestyle shoe that had the ability to sync with your iPod and keep track of your daily paces.

Following through with a multicoloured rainbow upper, which echoed HTM's original Woven (opposite), this model was released in a limited number and only available at Tier Zero stores.

SHOE DATA
EDITION
Tier Zero
YEAR RELEASED
2010
ORIGINAL PURPOSE
Lifestyle
TECHNOLOGY
Woven; Lunarlon; Nike+

NIKE AIR MAX 1
x ATMOS

THE BEST OF THE ATMOS AM1

The abundance of Air Max 1s released over the years makes this one of Nike's most popular models for collaborations; these applications from Japanese sneaker retailer Atmos are prime examples of the Air Max 1 done right.

SHOE DATA

EDITION
'Viotech' Air Max 1
PACK
'Atmos'
YEAR RELEASED
2003
ORIGINAL PURPOSE
Running
TECHNOLOGY
Max Air

SHOE DATA

EDITION
'Safari' Air Max 1
PACK
'Atmos'
YEAR RELEASED
2002
ORIGINAL PURPOSE
Running
TECHNOLOGY
Max Air

'SAFARI'

Atmos designed the first Air Max 1 to feature the Air Safari's signature print patterns. This extremely well-constructed sneaker features a combination of a durable canvas twill toe box, premium suede lace stays and a safari-print heel counter, ensuring exceptional wearability.

'VIOTECH'

Atmos's second Air Max 1 collaboration found favour for its earthy tones contained within a mix of leather and suede, and the 'Viotech' coloured Swoosh, which was reminiscent of early 90s ACG classics. The gum sole and subtle pops of gold stitching only added to the appeal.

'JADE'

This 2007 Quickstrike release saw Atmos take another iconic Nike print, this time cement, and apply it to the mudguard and heel collar of the Air Max 1. Using black and white throughout, the highlight colour was 'Jade', making this very similar to the extremely popular 'Tiffany Diamond' colourway seen on the Dunk Low Pro SB accents.

SHOE DATA

EDITION
'Jade' Air Max 1
PACK
'Atmos Quickstrike'
YEAR RELEASED
2007
ORIGINAL PURPOSE
Running
TECHNOLOGY
Max Air

NIKE AIR MAX 1 x KIDROBOT x BARNEYS

BARNEYS DOES THE ROBOT

Kidrobot, pioneer of limited edition art, toys, apparel and accessories, was the creative mastermind behind this release.

In true Kidrobot style, the shoe featured Pop art and mass-culture influences. It was sold exclusively at US department store Barneys.

Paul Budnitz and Chad Phillips of Kidrobot created a black/gold/pink colourway for this limited edition, and each pair came packaged in a specially designed gold-and-pink box that included a Kidrobot keychain.

Artists Gary Baseman, Dalek, David Horvath, Huck Gee and Frank Kozik created the designs on the custom innersoles. As only 200 pairs were made, these shoes remain highly collectable.

SHOE DATA

EDITION
Kidrobot
YEAR RELEASED
2005
ORIGINAL PURPOSE
Running
TECHNOLOGY
Max Air
EXTRAS
Extra innersoles;
Kidrobot keychain

NIKE AIR MAX 1 NL PREMIUM
'KISS OF DEATH' x CLOT

CHANNELLING THE CHI

Hong Kong-based CLOT enlisted the talents of artist MC Yan to help execute this stunningly detailed sneaker that articulates the foot's influence on the human body.

According to Chinese medicine, *Yongquan* is our most important pressure point because it transfers chi between earth and the body. On this shoe, the location of *Yongquan* was revealed in a diagram visible through the transparent outsole. A meridian map of the lower limb was drawn onto Chinese calligraphy paper and depicted on the Max 1's innersole.

The upper exposed the importance of the foot via a transparent toe box, the first seen on an Air Max 1. The vibrant use of orange and red with snakeskin and ostrich detailing gave the shoe a dynamic energy.

All this was encased within a fold-away box, similar to the boxes in which Chinese medical texts have traditionally been kept. A seal on the box signified authority; the graffiti-style text spelled out 'Hong Kong'.

NIKE AIR MAX x PATTA

COLLAB KINGS FLOATING ON AIR

Patta, pioneer of street culture, has a long line of Nike collaborations under its belt, and it all began with an Air Max 1 that represented the store's home turf of Amsterdam. Dutch illustrator Parra showcased his 'Amsterdam is King' logo on the 'AMS' Air Max 1, using a unique burgundy/pink/blue colourway inspired by the city's red-light district (shown here in the centre).

Next in line was the Air Max 90, made to coincide with the launch of Dutch hip-hop website State Magazine's *Homegrown* compilation album. The album's artwork was translated onto the Air Max 90 with a design based on a leafy, medicinal homegrown theme (bottom left).

Patta's 5th anniversary saw the launch of a further succession of Air Max 1s; the first two paid homage to the original Air Max 1 colourway (white/purple and white/green, shown top centre and top right), while the next two utilized darker shades of black and deep blue with green and red accents (centre right). All four used different hard-wearing materials, but were tied together with matching sockliners displaying artwork based on the five-guilder coin, and all featured the mini-Swoosh: The fifth Air Max 1 (centre left) saw the return of Parra as co-collaborator: tonal cherry was applied to a terry chenille, suede and mesh upper, with brighter designs on the outsole, insole and signature on the tongue.

SHOE DATA

EDITION
Patta
YEAR RELEASED
2005–10
ORIGINAL PURPOSE
Running
TECHNOLOGY
Max Air
EXTRAS
Extra laces

NIKE AIR MAX 90 'TONGUE N' CHEEK'
x DIZZEE RASCAL x BEN DRURY

CLASSIC AIR MAX GETS
THE BONKERS TREATMENT

This London exclusive was devised by the minds of two British creative forces and occasional collaborators: rapper Dizzee Rascal and seminal UK graphic designer Ben Drury.

Together the pair created this Air Max 90 to coincide with the release of Dizzee's LP *Tongue N' Cheek*, with Drury's artwork featuring on both album cover and sneaker design.

The shoe featured an embroidered tongue, the Dirtee Stank Recordings fly logo beneath the clear sole, and the Rascal's figure embossed on a 3M heel patch.

It was constructed from a subtle combination of chalk-white, premium leather and high-knap premium suede, accented with colours that reflected the album's artwork.

SHOE DATA

EDITION
'Tongue N' Cheek'
YEAR RELEASED
2009
ORIGINAL PURPOSE
Running
TECHNOLOGY
Max Air

NIKE AIR MAX 90 x KAWS

FOREVER 'XX'

In 2008 New York-based artist KAWS teamed up with Nike to bestow his trademark 'XX' on the Air Max 90.

Simplicity is KAWS' hallmark; keeping the canvas clean and white, he accentuated the sneaker's unique point of difference: its textures.

Leather side panels and linen inserts were partnered with a unique four-way stretch mesh toe, while striking flashes of volt green highlighted KAWS' cross-stitched 'XX' around the toe box, tongue, laces and outsole.

The KAWS x Nike drop also included an Air Max 90 Current coloured up in black with volt-green accents. The colour combination was a flip on the KAWS Air Force 1, which had been released for Nike's 1World project earlier that year.

Only 200 pairs were released.

SHOE DATA
EDITION
KAWS
YEAR RELEASED
2008
ORIGINAL PURPOSE
Running
TECHNOLOGY
Max Air

NIKE AIR MAX 90 x DQM 'BACONS'

THE FORERUNNER OF PREMIUM HYPERSTRIKE RELEASES

When the DQM (Dave's Quality Meat) store and brand were launched in New York City in 2003, savvy individuals knew that something good was coming to the streets. With a background in skateboarding, cycling, graffiti, music, art and many other elements of street culture, the founders' knowledge and creative nous has resulted in some of the best collaborative sneakers.

As one of the most-loved shoes ever, the Nike Air Max 90 was a perfect platter for DQM to serve up their creative wares. Following the store's butchering theme, DQM applied meat-inspired colours to the shoe, resulting in a totally unique piece of footwear that is lauded by many as the best Air Max colourway of all time.

The regular Quickstrike edition is hard enough to find today, but the Hyperstrike edition pictured here, limited to twenty-four pairs, featured a special tongue label, 'burnt' leather uppers and a bone print on the insole.

A T-shirt and special shoebox were also included as part of this friends and family release.

SHOE DATA

EDITION
Hyperstrike
EDITION
'Dave's Quality Meat'
YEAR RELEASED
2004
ORIGINAL PURPOSE
Running
TECHNOLOGY
Max Air
EXTRAS
T-shirt; extra laces;
plaster

NIKE AIR MAX 90 CURRENT HUARACHE x DQM

AIR MAX 90 CURRENT HUARACHE

DQM

0 200009 003082

USE BY
19.10.09

0.300   299.96   89.99
WEIGHT   PRICE PER   PRICE

BRINGING HOME THE BACON

This Nike Quickstrike offering, produced in conjunction with Dave's Quality Meat, re-used the colourway of one of the most popular Air Max 90 releases to date, and revisited the meat concept behind the New York sneaker mecca.

By combining elements from three of its most technologically successful running shoes – the Air Max 90, Air Huarache and Air Current – Nike created a hybrid silhouette that was more than the sum of its parts.

It featured the well-known bacon-inspired colour blocking, Thinsulate insulation and a 'Nike East' stamp on the tongue.

SHOE DATA

EDITION
Quickstrike
PACK
'Dave's Quality Meat'
YEAR RELEASED
2009
ORIGINAL PURPOSE
Running
TECHNOLOGY
Air Max 90 Current;
Huarache; Flywire;
Thinsulate
EXTRAS
x2 extra laces

NIKE AIR MAX 90 CURRENT MOIRE **QUICKSTRIKE**

MOIRE MEETS A MIX OF TECHNOLOGIES

For its Air Max 90 Current Moire, Nike integrated aspects of the Air Zoom Moire, Air Current and Air Max 90.

This hybrid approach took the best comfort technology from each model to realize one extremely comfortable silhouette.

The perforated one-piece, Moire-inspired upper allowed the foot to move naturally while remaining well ventilated.

Stitches outlined the Air Max 90's familiar panelling. The outsole was formed of half an Air Max unit to cushion the heel and Air Current sole technology that allowed the forefoot to flex freely.

The colourways were reminiscent of the first ever Tier Zero Air Zoom Moires released back in 2006, minus the speckled sole.

SHOE DATA
EDITION
Quickstrike
YEAR RELEASED
2008
ORIGINAL PURPOSE
Running
TECHNOLOGY
Air Max 90 Current;
Moire

SHOE DATA
EDITION
Unreleased sample
PACK
'Air You Breathe'
YEAR RELEASED
2006
ORIGINAL PURPOSE
Running
TECHNOLOGY
Max Air

NIKE x **BEN DRURY**

FROM MO' WAX TO MO' MAX

Having launched his career as art director at seminal UK record label Mo' Wax, by 2006 Ben Drury had one of the most desired dunks under his belt: a collaboration with legendary graffiti artist Futura 2000, known as the 'Dunkle' (see page 147).

Celebrating the launch of the Air Max 360, Nike enlisted three well-established graphic designers to rework three classic Air unit silhouettes for the 'Air You Breathe' pack, with Ben Drury chosen to work on the Air Max 1. Inspired by the pirate radio scene in London, the design features 'Hold Tight' written across the 3M tongue, radio transmission signals spread across the heel counter and a pylon printed on the innersole. (More of the 'Air You Breathe' pack is found on page 133.)

The 2009 'Silent Listener' (bottom left) was said to have been released to mark the long-standing creative partnership between Drury, Dizzee Rascal and Nike Sportswear, 'joining the dots' between the three (the Dizzee Rascal Air Max 90 is featured on page 118). Based on Drury's love of roaming through London and the countryside around Dartmoor, the shoe's flexible Air Current sole was topped with a rugged, blue ballistic nylon upper. Drury's appreciation for 'magical' 3M led him to weave it through both the red and blue lace combinations. Only 125 pairs were produced worldwide; 1948 in London held the majority of the stock.

SHOE DATA
EDITION
'Silent Listener'
YEAR RELEASED
2009
ORIGINAL PURPOSE
Running
TECHNOLOGY
Air Max 90 Current;
Max Air

NIKE AIR MAX 95 'PROTOTYPE' x MITA SNEAKERS

BLACK AND NEON

Mita Sneakers took the iconic neon Air Max 95 and executed a simple variation, blacking out the inner lining and tongue. Original Air Max 95 branding featured on the innersole, and 'Ueno' was embroidered on the inner lining – the district where the Mita boutique is situated in Tokyo.

This take on the neon colourway was first developed by Air Max 95 creator Sergio Lozano; in photographs of his desk that featured in a Q&A with the man himself in a Japanese magazine (called *Boon*), this sneaker is seen as a prototype sample, sitting alongside his initial sketches of it. This rendition was never released until 2013, hence its 'Prototype' moniker.

SHOE DATA

EDITION
Mita Sneakers
PACK
'Prototype'
YEAR RELEASED
2013
ORIGINAL PURPOSE
Running
TECHNOLOGY
Max Air; ghillie lacing

NIKE AIR 'NEON PACK'
x DAVE WHITE

WARNING: WET PAINT

British artist Dave White worked with Nike to release the 'Neon Pack' in 2005. It paid homage to the original Air Max 95 'Neon' in a 10th anniversary celebration.

The pack contained three pairs of sneakers (below, from left to right): Air Max 95, Air Max 90 and Air Max 1. The 1 and 90 featured the instantly recognizable classic neon/grey colour scheme found on the original Air Max 95. The felt-like material used across the upper, and the mesh around the top of the upper, were the same as those found on the first 95.

The 95 drew attention to its neon accents – on the Swoosh branding, Air bubbles and the laces – as they were applied to a white premium-leather upper.

Dave White revisited the neon theme in 2010 as part of the Size? 10th anniversary celebrations. The Nike Air Stab, released in the now infamous 'Neon' colourway in a run of just 400 pairs, was based on a painting of the silhouette produced at the time of the first 'Neon' drop. Shown here (below, far right) is the unreleased Air Stab sample that Dave White painted on the launch night.

SHOE DATA

EDITION
Size? exclusive
PACK
'Neon Pack'
YEAR RELEASED
2005
ORIGINAL PURPOSE
Running
TECHNOLOGY
Max Air; Footbridge (Stab); ghillie lacing
EXTRAS
Extra laces

NIKE AIR 180 x OPIUM

THE OPIUM EFFECT

The futuristic Opium store in Paris has
been an emporium for Nike and Air Jordan
since the year 2000, not only stocking
Tier Zero product, but also keeping some
of Nike's rarest sneakers on display.

In 2005, when Nike decided to bring
back 1991's Air 180, Opium was chosen
to launch it. This collaboration, featuring
the first Air 180 to be reissued in a new
colourway, generated much excitement.
The Opium make-up consisted of a
laser-etched camouflage heel and black
premium-leather upper.

A Hyperstrike version was also released,
which had faux snakeskin on the front
panelling, framing a purple toe box and
camouflage heel counter.

SHOE DATA

EDITION
Opium
YEAR RELEASED
2005
ORIGINAL PURPOSE
Running
TECHNOLOGY
Air 180; laser
EXTRAS
Extra laces

NIKE LUNAR AIR 180 ACG x SIZE?

SHOE DATA

EDITION
Size? only
PACK
'Lunar Air 180'
YEAR RELEASED
2010
ORIGINAL PURPOSE
Running
TECHNOLOGY
Lunarlon; Air 180;
no-sew; torch

**TRY THESE
ON FOR SIZE?**

To celebrate its 10th anniversary, Size? teamed up with Nike to bring together the classic running-shoe DNA of the Nike Air 180 with the outdoor stylings of its ACG range.

Using the Air 180 midsole and outsole as a starting point, Size? and Nike enhanced the shoe's performance by integrating ultra-light Lunarlon cushioning along the forefoot and a torch mesh panel underneath the no-sew upper.

What makes this sneaker a cut above other hybrids, however, is the application of colours and fabrics rekindled from the Air Terra, an ACG classic from circa 1991.

Limited to 300 pairs and only available in Size? stores in the UK, these were difficult to obtain on release and are still highly prized.

NIKE AIR FORCE 180 x **UNION**

AIR FORCE 180 GOES
AFRICAN SAFARI

One of the most memorable packs in Nike history, with releases during 2005 and 2006, 'Clerks' has included some of the sneaker world's best collaborations.

For this pack, store managers from some of the most influential shops in the world were invited to rework a Nike classic. The first leg showcased designs by Los Angeles-based retailers Stüssy, Undefeated and Union.

Union selected the Air Force 180, and, while the combination of safari print, a white/pink gradient and a yellow/blue/grey tongue might not appear to work on paper, the way the store's Chris Gibbs applied the colourway to the 90s basketball silhouette created a highly covetable sneaker.

SHOE DATA

EDITION
Union
PACK
'Clerks'
YEAR RELEASED
2005
ORIGINAL PURPOSE
Basketball
TECHNOLOGY
Air 180; hook-and-loop ankle strap

NIKE AIR MAX 97 360
x UNION 'ONE TIME ONLY'

A MERGING OF MODELS

In 2006 Nike introduced the Air Max 360, which boasted a full 360 sole air unit. To celebrate the inception of the new sole, Nike let loose the 'One Time Only' pack, which consisted of four hybrid Air Max models, each bestowed with a 360 air sole unit.

The design duo behind Nike's 'Clerks' pack and the brains behind this project, Richard Clarke and Jesse Leyva, chose four of their favourite 'Clerks' colourways for these new hybrid models.

Union's excellent colourway for the Air Force 180 was always odds-on to make the list, and was admirably applied to this Air Max 97 360 Tier Zero release.

SHOE DATA

EDITION
Union – Tier Zero
PACK
'One Time Only'
YEAR RELEASED
2006
ORIGINAL PURPOSE
Running
TECHNOLOGY
Max Air; ghillie lacing

SHOE DATA

EDITION
Slim Shady
PACK
'Artist Series'
YEAR RELEASED
2003
ORIGINAL PURPOSE
Running
TECHNOLOGY
Max Air

NIKE AIR BURST x SLIM SHADY

SHADY BURSTS ONTO THE SNEAKER SCENE

In 2003 Nike set up the Artist Series, collaborating with various artists from different disciplines such as Slim Shady, N.E.R.D., Halle Berry and Stash, each of whom was given the opportunity to rework their preferred model.

One of the most memorable sneakers came from Eminem with his Slim Shady Air Burst. It boasted a grey suede-and-mesh upper with leather accents throughout, an 'Air Slim Shady' tongue logo, 'E' on the lace jewel and insole, and the Shady Records logo on the translucent gum sole.

All proceeds from the Slim Shady Air Burst went to the Marshall Mathers Foundation, set up to provide funds to organizations working with troubled youths throughout the US.

SHOE DATA

EDITION
Slim Shady
PACK
'Eminem Charity
Series'
YEAR RELEASED
2006
ORIGINAL PURPOSE
Running
TECHNOLOGY
Max Air
EXTRAS
Certificate of
authenticity

131

NIKE AIR MAX 1 x SLIM SHADY

NO IMITATING THE REAL SLIM SHADY'S AUTOGRAPHED MODEL

After working with Nike on its Artist Series, Eminem teamed up with the sportswear giant again in 2006 to help raise funds for the Marshall Mathers Foundation.

He collaborated on a series of Air Max models that included the Air Max 1 (87), 90, 180, 93, 95, 97, 2003 and the Air Max 360, all of which were sold through auction at NikeTown London, Nike Berlin or on eBay. Eight pairs of each were produced. Only one pair of the Air Max 1s was available at NikeTown London, with the remaining seven sold on eBay.

The Air Max 1 was personally signed by the Real Slim Shady and featured a printed graphic of D12 member Big Proof, who passed away in 2006.

The shoes were individually numbered out of eight, and each pair came with a certificate of authenticity from the Marshall Mathers Foundation.

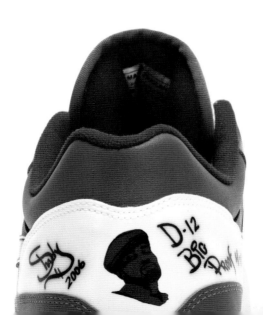

A STAB AT RESURRECTION

The Air Stab was rarely seen after its initial release in 1988, until London sneaker destination Footpatrol teamed up with Nike to rework the classic running silhouette.

The first release in 2005 saw black, purple, light blue and a touch of yellow on the upper, a very successful application that looked to have been inspired by a certain London transport upholstery colour scheme.

Initially sold exclusively at the Footpatrol store in London, these were later released to global Quickstrike accounts, much to the relief of many fans of the model.

Months later, a second Footpatrol Air Stab was released through Quickstrike accounts, featuring maple syrupy tones, with touches of yellow and light blue that linked it to the first release.

T-shirts and sticker packs were also produced to complete this highly acclaimed pack of Air Stabs.

SHOE DATA

EDITION
Quickstrike
YEAR RELEASED
2005
ORIGINAL PURPOSE
Running
TECHNOLOGY
Visible Air; Footbridge
EXTRAS
Mug; x2 laces; T-shirt; sticker pack; some boxes say 'Stabb' instead of 'Stab'

NIKE AIR STAB x HITOMI YOKOYAMA

SHOE DATA
EDITION
'Air You Breathe'
YEAR RELEASED
2006
ORIGINAL PURPOSE
Running
TECHNOLOGY
Visible Air; Footbridge
EXTRAS
Windrunner; T-shirt

YOKOYAMA PULLS A RABBIT OUT OF THE HAT

The Nike 'Air You Breathe' Quickstrike project featured collaborations with three artists: Kevin Lyons, Ben Drury and Hitomi Yokoyama. Each collection featured a T-shirt, windbreaker and pair of sneakers, all based around the concept of 'Air'.

UK-based Hitomi Yokoyama, known for her work with streetwear labels Gimme 5 and GOODENOUGH, worked on the Air Stab silhouette and produced a purple-hued interpretation.

The shoe also featured a bespoke rabbit icon that she designed to represent agility and fleet-footedness. The rabbit's paws were visible on the heeltab, while impressive colour blocking on the upper ensured that the shoe was both striking and memorable.

NIKE AIR CLASSIC BW & AIR MAX 95 x STASH

A NIKE-STASH CLASH: WE REMEMBER

Stash was one of the first artists to collaborate with Nike on the Artist Series in 2003, and his take on the Air Classic BW was a defining moment in the burgeoning sneaker culture movement.

The materials on the upper drew inspiration from Nike's ACG range, using a water-resistant Clima-FIT fabric and a re-ground (recycled) rubber Swoosh alongside premium leather and nubuck panels. Each pair was individually numbered out of 1,000 and featured Stash's signature logo on the tongue, as well as artwork on the insole.

Multiple tones of blue were used throughout; this theme was then repeated on Stash's 'Blue Pack' collection in 2006, which consisted of an Air Max 95 and an Air Force 1 (page 136) that were both made up of the same colourway and materials. Just under 2,000 of these were produced.

SHOE DATA

EDITION
Stash
PACK
'Artist Series'
YEAR RELEASED
2003
ORIGINAL PURPOSE
Running
TECHNOLOGY
Max Air;
Clima-FIT
EXTRAS
Hang tag,
slide-out box

SHOE DATA

EDITION
Stash
PACK
'Blue Pack'
YEAR RELEASED
2006
ORIGINAL PURPOSE
Running
TECHNOLOGY
Max Air

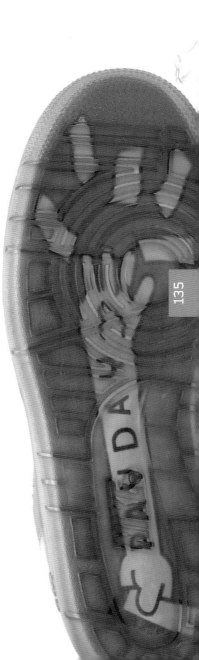

NIKE AIR FORCE II x ESPO

THE CLEAR ORIGINATOR

Known for his graffiti work during the 90s in Philadelphia and New York, Steve Powers, aka ESPO (Exterior Surface Painting Outreach), was infamous for putting his mark on various buildings, billboards and storefront shutters that were either blank or previously covered in someone else's work, normally marking them in black-and-white ESPO lettering.

ESPO's take on the Air Force II was the first sneaker to use clear panels for the upper. The model also featured reflective 3M panels and ESPO's artwork on the heel and insole. Every pair came with a bespoke pair of socks to be worn with the sneakers. Funds from the sales were donated to God's Love We Deliver, the artist's choice of charity, which provides meals to those in need.

SHOE DATA

EDITION
ESPO
PACK
'Artist Series'
YEAR RELEASED
2004
ORIGINAL PURPOSE
Basketball
TECHNOLOGY
Air; ghillie lacing
EXTRAS
Socks; hang tag

FORCES TO BE RECKONED WITH

We touched on a few limited edition collaborative models of the Air Force 1 – arguably one of Nike's all-time greatest models – in our first *Collectors' Guide*. Since then the surge of limited editions and collaborations focused on the model has been overwhelming.

Having celebrated its 25th and 30th anniversaries, the Air Force 1 has been modified with numerous technologies, materials and colourways, as well as being popular at custom design outlet NIKEiD. For many, however, the Air Force 1 will never get better than the white-on-white. Subtle plays on this have been achieved, including the ultra-clean one-piece 2005 edition (shoe no. 3, opposite). Here we have a selection of the best of the best.

1: AF-X Mid x Stash/Recon
2: Air Force 1 Supreme x ?uestlove
3: Air Force 1 LTD '1 Piece'
4: Air Force 1 '03 x Huf 'Hufquake'
5: AF-X Mid x Stash/Recon
6: Air Force 1 Supreme x Alife Rivington Club
7: Air Force 1 Supreme x Krink (Hyperstrike)
8: Air Force 1 Lux '07 'Crocodile'
9: Air Force 1 LA '03 x Mr Cartoon (Quickstrike)
10: Air Force 1 'Year Of The Dog' (Tier Zero)
11: Air Force 1 Premium x Stash
12: Air Force 1 Supreme x Krink
13: Air Force 1 Supreme Max Air x Nitraid
14: Air Force 1 x Livestrong x Mr Cartoon (Tier Zero)
15: Air Force 1 x HTM 'Croc'
16: Air Force 1 Lux max Air 'Pearl Collection'
17: Air Force 1 Supreme 'Year Of The Rabbit'
18: Air Force 1 Premium 'Invisible Woman'
19: Air Force 1 x Mr Cartoon 'Brown Pride'
20: Air Force 1 High Premium x Bobbito 'Mac 'N' Cheese'

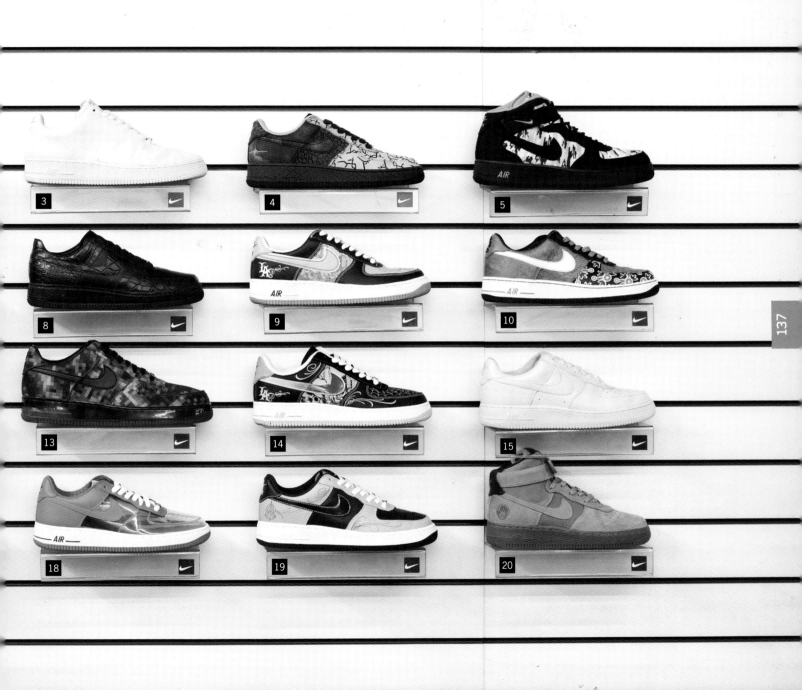

NIKE AIR FORCE 1
FOAMPOSITE
'TIER ZERO'

A COMPOSITE OF AIR FORCE AND FOAMPOSITE

Over the three decades since its initial release, the Air Force 1 has gone through numerous changes, but not many of the variations live up to the Foamposite fusion.

This Air Force 1 was given a full technological makeover when two of Nike's innovative shoes collided to make the Nike Air Force 1 Foamposite Tier Zero, combining the old school with new.

Foamposite technology reduced the number of layers of material needed to make up the Air Force 1, making the shoe more lightweight and the upper more supportive, and also provided a greater level of performance, durability, support and protection.

The seamless metallic silver design and translucent sole gave a futuristic look that highlighted the radical two-mould Foamposite process.

This edition was released on the weekend of the World Basketball Festival in August 2010.

SHOE DATA
EDITION
Foamposite 'Tier Zero'
YEAR RELEASED
2010
ORIGINAL PURPOSE
Basketball
TECHNOLOGY
Air; Foamposite; hook-and-loop ankle strap

NIKE AIR FOAMPOSITE ONE 'GALAXY'

OUT OF THIS WORLD

The Foamposite, Nike's signature sneaker for basketball star 'Penny' Hardaway, attracted little attention when first released in 1997 – perhaps ahead of its time – and the head-turning technology never really caught on.

In 2012, to commemorate Penny's return to Orlando playing in the NBA Celebrity All-Star Game, Nike released an extremely limited number of Foamposites in the now infamous 'Galaxy' colourway.

Around 500 people showed up at most stores to purchase the sneakers, which retailed for $220. The release attracted police attention after orderly queues turned frantic overnight.

The futuristic, galactic-themed, glow-in-the-dark-soled sneaker has become an instant classic and is highly sought after on sneaker auction sites.

SHOE DATA

EDITION
'Galaxy'
YEAR RELEASED
2012
ORIGINAL PURPOSE
Basketball
TECHNOLOGY
Air; Foamposite

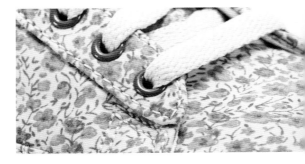

NIKE BLAZER x LIBERTY

A FORAY INTO FLORAL

The partnership between Nike and Liberty, London's world-renowned department store, has been a long and fruitful one.

Following the success of 2008's Nike Dunk, the Liberty Blazer was released on Valentine's Day 2009, and this one was just for the ladies.

Nike blessed the Blazer – the first basketball shoe that Nike produced, back in the early 70s – with one of Liberty's iconic fabrics, featuring an all-over floral print entitled 'Phoebe'. It was an interesting contrast to the usually plain make-ups seen on this clean-cut model.

SHOE DATA

EDITION
Liberty
YEAR RELEASED
2009
ORIGINAL PURPOSE
Basketball
TECHNOLOGY
Vulcanized sole;
herringbone sole

NIKE SB BLAZER x SUPREME

FLASH AND BRASH

The Nike Blazer has been around for a long while now – over four decades – and it continues to be a wardrobe staple. Nike worked with iconic retailer Supreme to deliver an interpretation of the SB Blazer, differing from its basketball forefather and adapted for skateboarding by adding extra padding around the collar and tongue, with the addition of a Zoom Air innersole.

Available in three colourways of red, black and white, each shoe featured a wide python-print Swoosh in grey, and an ode to bling in the form of a Gucci-inspired canvas ribbon detail and gold metal D-ring on the heel. The quilted-leather upper added to the overall premium feel.

The sneakers had people camping outside the Supreme store on their release, and they are still popular today.

SHOE DATA
EDITION
Supreme
YEAR RELEASED
2006
ORIGINAL PURPOSE
Skateboarding
TECHNOLOGY
Vulcanized sole;
herringbone sole;
Zoom Air
EXTRAS
x2 extra laces

NIKE VANDAL x APARTMENT STORE 'BERLIN'

BERLIN HYPE

SHOE DATA

EDITION
Hyperstrike
PACK
Apartment Store 'Berlin'
YEAR RELEASED
2003
ORIGINAL PURPOSE
Basketball
TECHNOLOGY
**Hook-and-loop
ankle strap;
pivot point**

Berlin's Apartment store isn't well known today for a Nike release; but back in 2003 the underground high-fashion store discreetly produced a Hyperstrike Vandal in an extremely limited run.

With only twenty-four pairs distributed among friends, family and the odd passer-by, these have rarely been seen in the wild. As we wrote this book, there was a pair going on a popular auction site at a 'Buy it now' price of $5,000...

The 80s design was kept real with an OG Vandal-style colour-up on a nylon canvas, with a black/grey/hot pink combination that had never been seen on a Vandal.

Details came in the shape of an embroidered Fernsehturm tower on the heel, 'Berlin' embroidered on the heeltab and the Apartment label stitched behind the tongue.

VANDAL: A PERSON WHO DESTROYS WHAT IS BEAUTIFUL

For his interpretation of the Vandal, Los Angeles-based artist Geoff McFetridge took the name of the model literally.

When first purchased, these sneakers appeared flawless and well laundered, with pinstripe cotton balanced by taped seams.

But once the cotton canvas started to wear away, or was defaced, Geoff's graphic artwork was revealed, featuring the words 'I just can't stop destroying'.

The underlying white-and-silver graphic print complemented the Geoff McFetridge 'teeth' emblem on the heeltab.

These were also available in white and olive green.

NIKE VANDAL SUPREME
'TEAR AWAY' x GEOFF McFETRIDGE

SHOE DATA

EDITION
Geoff McFetridge
YEAR RELEASED
2003
ORIGINAL PURPOSE
Basketball
TECHNOLOGY
Hook-and-loop
ankle strap;
pivot point
EXTRAS
Extra laces

143

NIKE TENNIS CLASSIC AC TZ
'MUSEUM' x CLOT

SHOE DATA

EDITION
Tier Zero
PACK
CLOT 'Museum'
YEAR RELEASED
2012
ORIGINAL PURPOSE
Tennis
TECHNOLOGY
Herringbone sole
EXTRAS
Chinese treasure box; sandpaper

CLOT'S FUTURE CLASSIC

For this collaboration, Hong Kong-based CLOT saw the simple clean lines of the Tennis Classic as the epitome of old-school vintage, and wanted to create a 'future throwback of now'.

Using a futuristic metallic silver upper, with red accents that symbolize good luck in Chinese culture, Edison Chen from CLOT asked his team to select one pair each; these numbered pairs were individually sanded down by hand to create a unique 'worn-in' effect, and then sold in a traditional Chinese treasure box. For those who didn't get their hands on a personalized edition, a sheet of sandpaper was supplied in the box, so they could to attempt their own reconstruction.

Edison Chen envisaged the Tennis Classic as a museum exhibit in fifty years' time, and this was reflected in the packaging and overall concept.

SHOE DATA
EDITION
Tier Zero
PACK
Wood Wood
YEAR RELEASED
2009
ORIGINAL PURPOSE
Outdoor running
TECHNOLOGY
Ion-mask;
Lunarlon; Dynamic
Support; Nike+

NIKE LUNARWOOD+
x WOOD WOOD

GONE WILD

Scandinavian retailer Wood Wood produced the Lunarwood, an updated version of the outdoor-styled Nike Wildwood for today's urban environment, featuring the revolutionary Lunarlon cushioning technology in conjunction with Dynamic Support technology.

For Wood Wood, a classic outdoor ACG silhouette was adapted for today's urban environments, while not forgetting the style cues that made the shoe a favourite in the first place. The upper consisted of ion-mask technology designed to keep the foot comfortable and dry, while the Lunarlon sole unit made this the ideal lightweight cushioned runner for fast, dynamic movement. Further details included a bold 'WW' on the left heel and a graphic of a full moon in eclipse illustrated on the sockliner, inspired by nocturnal bombing (graffiti) expeditions.

Released in a limited quantity at Tier Zero stores, this is a smooth and minimal modern interpretation of an ACG classic.

NIKE DUNK **EDITIONS**

DUNK DISTINCTIONS

The Dunk silhouette, in both high- and low-top versions, has been the base for a slew of collaborations since its birth in 1985.

N.E.R.D. fans adored Pharrell Williams's Artist Series Dunk, a slick black faux-reptilian high-top with red laces, of which just 1,050 individually numbered pairs were made; a rare one-off sample has been spotted online featuring full snakeskin upper, labelled '0000 of 1050'.

Undefeated's 2002 low-top splatter Dunks were groundbreaking with their unexpected colour choice and unique

pattern – only twenty-four pairs of the Hyperstrike edition shown here were produced, none of which were released to the general public. Two alternative colourways were distributed on a wider release.

The airbrushed, faded design of the 2003 Premium Haze dunk by Eric Haze (legendary NYC graffiti artist and designer whose work includes the Public Enemy and MTV logos) garnered much attention, with only 1,000 pairs made.

SHOE DATA

EDITION
Pharrell Williams
PACK
'Artist Series'
YEAR RELEASED
2004
ORIGINAL PURPOSE
Basketball
TECHNOLOGY
Pivot point

SHOE DATA

EDITION
Haze
YEAR RELEASED
2003
ORIGINAL PURPOSE
Basketball
TECHNOLOGY
Pivot point

SHOE DATA

EDITION
Hyperstrike
PACK
'Undefeated'
YEAR RELEASED
2002
ORIGINAL PURPOSE
Basketball
TECHNOLOGY
Pivot point

NIKE DUNK SB **EDITIONS**

FROM ALLEY-OOP TO OLLIE

Since 2002 Nike SB has unleashed a plethora of Dunk Pro SB sneakers, usually in conjunction with sponsored Nike Pro skaters or skate-affiliated brands and artists.

The Dunk's advancement from the original basketball to the skate version was all in the cushioning; a Zoom Air innersole was integrated into the sneaker.

The Dunk SB's emphasis was also on cushioning throughout its ankle collar and tongue, which was secured in place with elastic strapping.

The 'Dunkle' was conceived when UK record label Mo' Wax was set to release the second album from U.N.K.L.E.,

Never, Never, Land. The shoe featured graffiti artist Futura's artwork from the album cover, under the direction of Mo' Wax's joint art directors, Ben Drury and Will Bankhead. It was consequently nicknamed the 'U.N.K.L.E. Dunkle'.

Street artist Pushead also created an all-encompassing Dunk SB package, applying his artwork to the Dunk, box and hang tags, making the shoe all the more desirable.

SHOE DATA

EDITION
'U.N.K.L.E. DUNKLE'
PACK
Nike SB
YEAR RELEASED
2004
ORIGINAL PURPOSE
Skateboarding
TECHNOLOGY
Zoom Air; pivot point

SHOE DATA

EDITION
Pushead
PACK
Nike SB
YEAR RELEASED
2005
ORIGINAL PURPOSE
Skateboarding
TECHNOLOGY
Zoom Air; pivot point

FRANKENDUNK –
IT'S ALIVE!

Since 2002 Nike SB have been releasing successful, never re-released drops of limited edition SB Dunks. Nike acknowledged its accomplishments by selecting a piece or panel from every Dunk SB produced, and combined these elements Frankenstein-style to create the What The Dunk.

This extremely limited release in 2007 coincided with the Nike SB film, *Nothing But the Truth*, that had been three years in the making. We took it upon ourselves to decipher and break down this behemoth, photograph all the Dunks together and show where each element had come from. Unfortunately, a few Dunks eluded us including the very rare Medicom I, II and III.

This was, however, a good way of getting as many Dunk SBs on a spread as we could, as it is near to impossible to weigh up one against the other.

Each edition featured here is rare and covetable for different reasons. Their names don't necessarily reflect a direct collaboration; often they describe where the inspiration for the shoe came from, or how it is perceived.

SHOE DATA

EDITION
What The Dunk
PACK
Nike SB
YEAR RELEASED
2007
ORIGINAL PURPOSE
Skateboarding
TECHNOLOGY
Zoom Air; pivot point

LEFT FOOT (clockwise from top left)
Dunk Low Pro SB 'Paris' – 2003
Dunk Low Pro SB 'Heineken' – 2003
Dunk Low Pro SB 'Avengers' – 2005
Dunk Low Pro SB 'Shanghai' – 2004
Dunk High Pro SB 'Lucky 7' – 2004
Dunk High Pro SB 'Sea Crystal' – 2004
Dunk Low Pro SB 'Raygun' – 2005
Dunk High Pro SB x Supreme – 2003
Dunk Low Pro SB 'Cali' – 2004
Dunk High Pro SB 'Unlucky 13' – 2004
Dunk Low Pro SB x Supreme – 2002
Dunk Low Pro SB 'Red Hemp' – 2004
Dunk Low Pro SB 'Blue Hemp' – 2004
Dunk High Pro SB x Supreme – 2003
RIGHT FOOT (clockwise from top left)
Dunk High Pro SB x Supreme – 2003
Dunk Low Pro SB 'Jedi' – 2004
Dunk Low Pro SB 'Tiffany' – 2005
Dunk Low Pro SB 'Carhartt' – 2004
Dunk High Pro SB 'T-19' – 2005
Dunk Low Pro SB 'London' – 2004
Dunk Low Pro SB 'Tweed' – 2004
Dunk Low Pro SB 'Bison' – 2003
Dunk High Pro SB 'De La Soul' – 2005
Dunk High Pro SB 'Lucky 7' – 2004
Dunk Low Pro SB 'Oompa Loompa' – 2005
Dunk High Pro SB x Huf – 2004
Dunk Low Pro SB 'Shanghai II' – 2005
Dunk Low Pro SB 'Pigeon' – 2005
Dunk Low Pro SB 'Buck' – 2003
Dunk High Pro SB 'Daniel Shimizu' – 2004
Dunk Low Pro SB 'Reese Forbes' – 2004

x **SUPREME**

SHOE DATA
EDITION
Supreme
YEAR RELEASED
2009
ORIGINAL PURPOSE
Skateboarding
TECHNOLOGY
Zoom Air; herringbone sole
EXTRAS
Key ring; extra laces

150

BRINGING THE BRUIN INTO SB

Next in line for the skateboarding treatment of extra padding and Zoom Air integration was the 1972 Bruin, one of Nike's first low-top basketball sneakers. Supreme helped bring the Bruin to the skateboarding world in 2009 as Nike looked for a successor to the Blazer Low SB.

Presented in four colourways, the Nike Zoom Bruin SB featured typically Supreme-esque colour blocking – also respectful of the original Bruins – with all-over black, red, green or white uppers and matching laces contrasting against white midsoles. 'Nike World Famous' branding stood out on the heels, reminiscent of Supreme's own logo, while a metallic Swoosh continued the bling theme.

The sneakers came with a 'World Famous' key ring, and a matching twill pullover jacket was also available.

SHOE DATA

EDITION
Supreme
YEAR RELEASED
2008
ORIGINAL PURPOSE
Skateboarding
TECHNOLOGY
Zoom Air; supportive
forefoot strap
EXTRAS
Extra laces; varsity
baseball jacket

x SUPREME

FROM CROSS-TRAINING
TO SUPREME SKATING

The king of crossing over, Bo Jackson, was the first athlete to be named an All-Star in both American baseball and football; he was also Nike's front man for its line of Air Trainer cross trainers, 'Bo Knows'. One of the models in this family was the Air Trainer TW II (TW standing for 'Totally Washable'), which was a low-cut, more lightweight version of its predecessors. In 2008 Supreme joined forces with Nike to bring back this silhouette, which hadn't been reissued before, taking the Air Trainer and redesigning it from the ground up with skateboarding in mind.

Four colourways were produced with a clear outsole that revealed the Supreme logo across the bottom of the shoe. With no former lasts or tooling available, the Nike SB team rebuilt the Air Trainer TW II using the rugged last of the Air Trainer III as a base pattern, which resulted in improved construction while keeping the original aesthetics. However, suede panelling meant that these shoes were no longer 'Totally Washable'. The result was the Air Trainer II SB.

NIKE FLYKNIT x HTM

SUPER-FLY KNIT

Nike's breakthrough Flyknit showcased
the work of design trio HTM. Always
known to back the unexpected or
unorthodox Nike releases, such as the
Wovens (pages 110–11), HTM became
acquainted with Flyknit technology
and produced a plethora of unique
interpretations of the Lunar Flyknit
and Flyknit Racer.

The new-age technology aimed to make
running sneakers lighter, with less drag
for athletes; the engineered knit formed
one continuous layer, without the need
for multiple panels stitched together.

Shown here are some of the many HTM
releases of the Lunar Flyknit dropped in
instalments throughout 2012, as well
as the Flyknit Racer released to coincide
with the US track and field team's kit
colourway for the 2012 Olympic Games
(shown below, left and right).

Each edition was released in small
runs with 'HTM' woven into the tongue
for extra detail; some are also
individually numbered.

SHOE DATA

EDITION
Tier Zero
PACK
'HTM'
YEAR RELEASED
2012
ORIGINAL PURPOSE
Running
TECHNOLOGY
Flyknit; Flywire;
Lunarlon; Nike+

TAKING IT YEEZY

In 2009 Nike joined forces with Grammy award-winning recording artist Kanye West to design and create the first ever signature shoe by a non-athlete in Nike's history: the Nike Air Yeezy.

This shoe elevated sneaker hype to levels never witnessed before; the UK release was even picked up by some major national newspapers.

The Yeezy sported a full-grain leather upper and a remastered Air Assault outsole complete with glow-in-the-dark properties. Other details included a patent-leather forefoot support strap, a premium suede toe wrap feature with 'Y' embossed on it, and 'Yeezy' on the heel pull.

Three colourways of the Air Yeezy were known colloquially as the 'Zen Greys' (shown below, second from left), 'Nets' (centre) and 'Black and Pinks' (second from right).

The Yeezy II, released in 2012, celebrated the iconic Nike cross-training silhouettes; it was built on the Nike Air Tech Challenge II tennis shoe outsole, with the addition of a moulded forefoot strap.

An obsessive approach to materials resulted in a luxurious mix of leather, rugged ballistic nylon and soft nubuck.

Subtle Ancient Egyptian touches could be found throughout: the god Horus on the tongue; a loop strap with hieroglyphics that spelled out 'YZY'; each screw-on lace aglet was obelisk-shaped; and the anaconda texture was echoed on the eyelets and leather lace toggle that carried the Roman numeral 'II'.

The Air Yeezy II came in black/solar red (far left) and platinum/solar red (far right) editions.

154

SHOE DATA

EDITION
Quickstrike/NRG
PACK
Air Yeezy/Air Yeezy II
YEAR RELEASED
2009/2012
ORIGINAL PURPOSE
Lifestyle
TECHNOLOGY
Air Yeezy: Visible Air; supportive forefoot strap; pivot point; padded ankle collar
Air Yeezy II: Visible Air; supportive forefoot strap; herringbone sole; external heel counter; torch

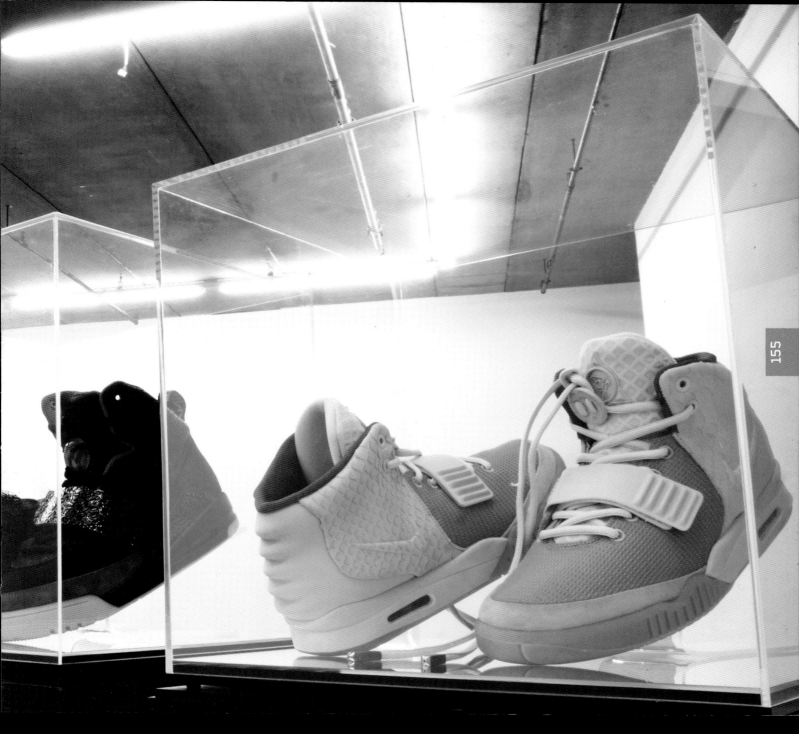

NIKE AIR MAG

MAG-NIFICENT AWARENESS FOR PARKINSON'S DISEASE

Originally designed by Nike luminary Tinker Hatfield in 1989, the Air Mag was worn by Michael J. Fox's character Marty McFly in the hit movie *Back to the Future Part II*. All the *Back to the Future* films are based in 1985; for this film, the directors approached Tinker to design a sneaker that looked like it had been made thirty years into the future.

After the movie's release, there was demand from sneaker enthusiasts for the shoe to be created for real, and so, after five years in the making, a model was made by Nike that was as close to the original as possible. The project was intended to increase awareness of Parkinson's disease and raise funds for the Michael J. Fox Foundation.

The shoe had an electroluminescent outsole powered by a rechargeable battery with a 3,000-hour life, and each charge could keep the sole unit illuminated for four hours. The model came in bespoke cardboard packaging with a magnetic closure system, certificate of authenticity, DVD, manual and lapel pin.

Only 1,500 pairs were made available via online auction site eBay.

SHOE DATA

EDITION
Air Mag
YEAR RELEASED
2011
ORIGINAL PURPOSE
Display only
TECHNOLOGY
Electroluminescent;
LED panel; Air;
rechargeable
EXTRAS
DVD with videos;
flyer/manual;
certificate of authenticity;
lapel pin; bespoke box

AIR JORDAN

It is hard to know where to begin when talk turns to Nike's Air Jordan, arguably the most important line in the history of sneakers.

Starting with basketball rookie Michael Jordan, who changed the game for ever, through to the fines imposed when he wore the 'banned' black/red Jordan Is on court, the legendary 'Mars Blackmon' Spike Lee commercials, and Tinker Hatfield's incredible Air Jordan III that convinced Michael to stay with Nike, the story is as interesting as the sneakers are great.

The Air Jordan line currently stands at twenty-three pairs, and has expanded to include a selection of other athletic footwear and apparel for a variety of sports. The range has been so successful that it has been repositioned as a standalone division of Nike and is today known simply as Jordan Brand.

Air Jordan is still a leader in sports performance, with a current line-up that includes NBA superstars Chris Paul and Carmelo Anthony (page 163), as well as baseball stars Derek Jeter and Jimmy Rollins, all representing the 'Jumpman'.

Reissues of popular early models such as the Air Jordan III and Air Jordan IV still generate instant queues of athletic footwear lovers eager to recapture a sneaker moment from their past, alongside newer fans of the brand who are attracted to its history and classic designs.

Jordan Brand has produced some outstanding collaborations and limited editions over the years. Typically, the Air Jordan III, Air Jordan IV and Air Jordan V models have caused the biggest frenzies in the limited edition marketplace. Even mash-ups of these earlier sneakers, such as the Spiz'ike – a collaboration between Spike Lee and Michael Jordan himself – have proved instantly popular.

Jordan Brand remains at the forefront of design, working with charities including The Doernbecher Children's Hospital Foundation, as well as making more traditional connections, for example with artists such as Dave White (page 172).

Notably, there is also the Air Jordan Bin 23 collection, which only showcases premium materials and executions across a selection of classic models.

SHOE DATA

EDITION
'Sole to Sole'
YEAR RELEASED
2009
ORIGINAL PURPOSE
Basketball
TECHNOLOGY
Air; hook-and-loop ankle
strap; pivot point

'SOLE TO SOLE'

MIDNIGHT MARAUDERS

The Air Jordan I High Strap rarely gets the limited edition treatment, so
when it was released in hard-to-get quantities in 2009, complete with
A Tribe Called Quest album artwork as the inspiration, there was little
surprise that it became a hit.

The upper consisted of a black canvas – not often seen on an Air Jordan
– combined with black tumbled-leather panelling and a patent black
Swoosh for added textural contrast. Red and green accents reflected
the seminal hip-hop group's 1993 *Midnight Marauders* cover artwork.
These were difficult to find, only being sold through 'urban accounts'.

'25TH ANNIVERSARY'

SILVER ANNIVERSARY SNEAKERS

What could be more befitting of a silver anniversary celebration than this Air Jordan I Retro High edition?

Released for the model's 25th year in 2010, this sneaker's upper utilizes a mix of grey nubuck and metallic silver foil leather, featuring on the tongue the interlocking '23/25' logo found on the Air Jordan 2010.

The sneakers came boxed in a special-edition foam-padded aluminium suitcase with the '23/25' graphic just under the handles; they were only available at select Jordan retailers worldwide.

161

SHOE DATA

EDITION
'25th Anniversary'
YEAR RELEASED
2010
ORIGINAL PURPOSE
Basketball
TECHNOLOGY
Air; pivot point
EXTRAS
Aluminium case

AIR JORDAN I RETRO HIGH
RUFF N TUFF 'QUAI 54'

LASER-BLUE AIR JORDAN Is TUMBLE ONTO THE COURT

In 2009 Jordan Brand hit Paris to host Quai 54, an annual outdoor basketball tournament featuring sixteen of the world's finest streetball teams, all competing for the Quai 54 Championship trophy.

To celebrate the event, Jordan Brand launched limited edition Air Jordan I and Jordan Element models as part of the 'Ruff N Tuff' collection.

The Air Jordan I consisted of a laser-blue wrinkled-leather upper with a black Swoosh and laces, and a white midsole covered in black speckles. Further details included white contrast stitching, a special 'Quai 54' tongue label and wild print lining. The pattern on the lining also appeared beneath the transparent outsole.

SHOE DATA

EDITION
Ruff N Tuff
'Quai 54'
YEAR RELEASED
2009
ORIGINAL PURPOSE
Basketball
TECHNOLOGY
Air; pivot point

SHOE DATA

EDITION
Carmelo Anthony
Player Edition
YEAR RELEASED
2004
ORIGINAL PURPOSE
Basketball
TECHNOLOGY
Air; pivot point;
external heel counter;
ghillie lacing
EXTRAS
Retro card

AIR JORDAN II 'CARMELO'

A LITTLE NUGGET BECOMES A BIG GEM

The Air Jordan II was the first and only Air Jordan not to feature any Swoosh branding, something rarely seen at the time. The initial low version was produced in 1986, followed by three editions of the high in 1987 and a further collection of both in 1995.

In 2004 Jordan Brand brought them back again, releasing numerous make-ups of the model throughout the year. One of the standout versions was Jordan Brand ambassador Carmelo Anthony's Denver Nuggets-inspired colourway.

The upper was made of the pebbled-leather and faux lizard-skin panels seen on the original versions, staying true to the heritage of the model. Pairs sold out almost instantly at stores lucky enough to stock them, making them one of the most highly prized Air Jordan II editions.

A black/blue 'Away' pair and a white/red/blue '2004 Olympic Games' pair were made bespoke for Carmelo; these were never made available to the public.

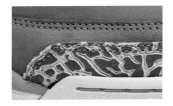

AIR JORDAN III 'DO THE RIGHT THING'

BUGGIN' OUT FOR JORDANS

Nike has had a close association with film director Spike Lee ever since the memorable series of Weiden+Kennedy-produced Air Jordan commercials that aired in the late 80s and early 90s. The character Mars Blackmon was created as part of the series and was portrayed by Lee himself.

Spike Lee's 1989 film *Do the Right Thing* provided the concept behind this Jordan III; the film garnered particular attention from sneakerheads thanks to a scene in which character Buggin' Out gets his Air Jordan IVs scuffed. Colours from the movie poster were used as inspiration for this limited edition US-only release.

The vibrant blue suede upper, matched with yellow detailing and the infamous cement print, made these a standout and highly desirable edition.

SHOE DATA
EDITION
'Do the Right Thing'
YEAR RELEASED
2007
ORIGINAL PURPOSE
Basketball
TECHNOLOGY
Visible Air; pivot point;
external heel counter;
ghillie lacing

AIR JORDAN III WHITE 'FLIP'

FLIP IT GOOD

The Air Jordan III is one of the most popular Air Jordan signature models, and continues to resonate today with Jordan lovers everywhere.

It was the first Jordan to feature a visible air unit, cement print and the 'Jumpman' logo. Also adding to its infamy was the 1988 All-Star Weekend in Chicago, during which Michael Jordan flew in from the free throw line to defend his championship against Dominique Wilkins and win the Slam Dunk contest while wearing the Air Jordan III.

In 2006 Jordan brand wanted to 'flip' things a little, so it revisited the original 1988 white/cement Air Jordan III and inverted the detailing on the panels, putting emphasis on the already well-known cement print that was usually seen on the toe guard and heel.

This release was a hit with fans of the brand, and was a must-have addition to the collections of Jordan Brand connoisseurs.

AIR JORDAN IV
RETRO RARE AIR 'LASER'

LASER ETCHING AT ITS BEST

This Air Jordan IV Rare Air was based on the 1989 black/cement-grey version, with the addition of a laser-etched leather upper, red laces and a 3M back panel.

This was the second Air Jordan to feature laser-etched detailing; the Air Jordan XX was the first. The fire-red colourway of the IV from 1989 was also included in the pack and featured the same laser etching.

The Air Jordan IV Retro Rare Air 'Laser' was a Quickstrike release that sold out quickly at select Jordan Brand accounts.

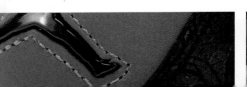

SHOE DATA

EDITION
Rare Air
PACK
'Laser'
YEAR RELEASED
2005
ORIGINAL PURPOSE
Basketball
TECHNOLOGY
**Visible Air; laser;
herringbone sole**

AIR JORDAN IV
'MARS BLACKMON'

BLACKMON-BRANDED MAKES ALL THE DIFFERENCE

Well known among fans of Jordan Brand, Spike Lee, aka Mars Blackmon (the name of his Brooklyn character in the 1986 film *She's Gotta Have It*), featured in several Nike adverts, including one for the 1989 Air Jordan IV.

Due to the overwhelming popularity of the original fire-red colourway from 1989 and the success of the 'Rare Air' laser-etched version that came out in 2005, Jordan Brand released a version with Mars Blackmon branding on the ankle in 2006. This edition stayed as true to the original as possible, with the exception of the 'Jumpman' logo that replaced the Nike Air branding on the heel, the TPU top and bottom eyelets and, of course, the laser-etched Mars Blackmon logo.

SHOE DATA

EDITION
'Mars Blackmon'
YEAR RELEASED
2006
ORIGINAL PURPOSE
Basketball
TECHNOLOGY
Visible Air; laser

AIR JORDAN V RETRO RARE AIR 'LASER'

SHOE DATA

EDITION
Rare Air
PACK
'Laser'
YEAR RELEASED
2007
ORIGINAL PURPOSE
Basketball
TECHNOLOGY
Visible Air; laser;
herringbone sole;
padded ankle support
EXTRAS
Retro card

SHARP SHOOTERS

With the Air Jordan IV Rare Air 'Laser' an
instant hit, Jordan Brand took note and
decided to continue with the laser concept,
incorporating the Air Jordan V into the series.

The highly intricate laser designs stood
out against the white upper, while the
bright orange midsole and green shark
teeth speckled with metallic flakes worked
alongside the 3M tongue embellished with
an orange 'Jumpman'.

The inner lining also featured detailed
designs of various Air Jordans depicted in
the same orange/olive colourway, which
complemented the concept and rounded
out the model.

AIR JORDAN V RETRO 'QUAI 54'

NO COMPETITION

Quai 54 is a French streetball tournament sponsored by Jordan Brand, which has celebrated the annual event in Paris through the release of limited edition Air Jordans.

Various Air Jordan models have had a Quai 54 makeover over the years, including the I (page 162), IV, IX and Team ISO 2, some of which were never released to the public.

These Air Jordan Vs featured a simple yet memorable colourway. The white tumbled-leather upper had black and green accents and 'Quai 54' branding on the heel panel, which matched the black midsole and translucent green outsole. They were available exclusively at Footlocker Europe and House Of Hoop stores, and in a raffle at the Nike store in Harajuku, Japan.

A black/green version was also produced for friends and family, limited to fifty-four pairs.

SHOE DATA

EDITION
'Quai 54'
YEAR RELEASED
2011
ORIGINAL PURPOSE
Basketball
TECHNOLOGY
Visible Air; herringbone sole;
padded ankle support

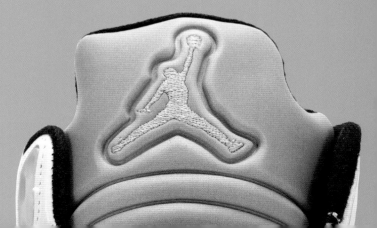

AIR JORDAN V
'GREEN BEANS'

SHOE DATA

EDITION
Green Beans
YEAR RELEASED
2006
ORIGINAL PURPOSE
Basketball
TECHNOLOGY
**Visible Air;
herringbone sole;
padded ankle support**

GREEN BEANS: THEY'RE GOOD FOR YOU

When Tinker Hatfield originally designed the Air Jordan V, he drew inspiration from Second World War Mustang fighter planes to reference Michael Jordan's game style – specifically the way he would effortlessly overpower opponents.

Since the inception of the model in 1990, it has seen several make-ups, though few have been as memorable as the 'Green Bean', for which the 3M fabric used on all Air Jordan V tongues was extended to cover the whole upper, then contrasted with green accents and trim; it was an instant classic.

AIR JORDAN V T23 'JAPAN ONLY'

ONE FOR JAPAN'S EYES ONLY

In May 2011 Jordan Brand and XBS (director of clothing brand Nitraid and member of Japanese hip-hop group Nitro Microphone Underground) hosted the Jordan Tokyo 23 basketball tournament.

To celebrate the event, Jordan Brand released its first collection of products exclusive to Japan; this included two T-shirts, a pair of Jordan CP3 IVs and the extremely limited Air Jordan V T23, all of which were made in conjunction with XBS.

The Air Jordan V T23 featured a predominantly yellow nubuck upper with

'Tokyo' embroidered in Kanji lettering on the outer heel panel, black and grey accents throughout the shoe, and speckled teeth on the midsole above the clear rubber outsole.

These have gone on to become one of the rarest and most in-demand Air Jordans ever produced.

SHOE DATA

EDITION
T23
PACK
'Japan Only'
YEAR RELEASED
2011
ORIGINAL PURPOSE
Basketball
TECHNOLOGY
**Visible Air;
herringbone sole;
padded ankle support**

AIR JORDAN I
'WINGS FOR THE FUTURE' x DAVE WHITE

A LOVE THAT GOES WAY BACK

The year 2011 saw UK artist Dave White and Jordan Brand release their collaborative take on the Air Jordan I in time for the NBA All-Star Weekend. This extremely limited edition featured a stars-and-stripes motif around the panels, as well as a gradient gold design stretching from the leather toe box up to Dave's signature splatter-effect side panel. Only twenty-three pairs were produced, in a nod to Michael Jordan's player number, and Sole Collector hosted an online auction for the release with all proceeds going to Jordan Brand's charitable WINGS for the Future programme.

A year later the duo released another version to the hungry public, inspiring hundreds of people to queue up to purchase a pair. Most noticeable in the avant-garde design was the removal of the Swoosh from the upper altogether.

Numerous sample versions were produced in the run-up to the final release, as White filtered through a selection of materials and colours, including various grains of leather, nubuck, 3M, removable Swooshes and bubble wing branding on the ankle panel.

SHOE DATA

EDITION
Dave White
YEAR RELEASED
2011/2012
ORIGINAL PURPOSE
Basketball
TECHNOLOGY
Air; pivot point
EXTRAS
Special box

PUMA

The brand with the 'Formstripe' was founded in 1948 in Herzogenaurach, Germany, by Rudolf Dassler following a bitter feud with his brother, Adi Dassler, who went on to found adidas.

Over the years Puma has positioned itself as one of the world leaders in athletic footwear and apparel in both lifestyle and performance applications.

Its sneakers are seen on the feet of the world's fastest man, Usain Bolt, while the brand has also been integral to hip-hop and breakdancing culture for the last three decades. Basketball silhouettes such as

the Puma Clydes, States and Suedes have now become style icons in their own right.

This positioning of Puma as a cultural touchpoint across a range of urban subcultures has ensured that it stays in the public eye and plays a prominent part in the culture of athletic footwear.

Puma has also been quick to recognize the potential of the market for limited editions, and was quick to open its archives, with impressive results quickly following. Obvious partnerships, such as the *YO! MTV Raps* collaboration (pages 178–79), which

paid homage to hip-hop, have been a success alongside more sneaker-centric stories, such as the Clyde x Undefeated 'Snakeskin' pack (page 181) that dropped to huge acclaim. Releases such as the Suede Classic x Shinzo 'Usain Bolt' (page 182) also highlight the way in which the brand is prepared to combine lifestyle and performance stories to great effect.

Top-tier line The List is now home to the most limited of Puma editions.

PUMA STATES
x SOLEBOX

STATE-OF-THE-ART ADD-ONS

As a part of its 10th anniversary celebrations, Berlin-based retailer Solebox showcased its strong relationship with Puma by releasing three pairs of exclusive Puma States.

Based on its first Puma collaboration – the Clyde, back in 2007 – Solebox made use of similar features, including a suede upper and snakeskin detailing on the Formstripe.

Other special details include a dual-branded tongue label, a Solebox lace jewel and Solebox branded lace tips, as well as a leather lace pouch (also seen in the Shadow Society pack on page 185) with a dual-branded label.

Each version was limited to 100 pairs and was only sold through Solebox, both in-store and online.

SHOE DATA
EDITION
Solebox
PACK
'Snakeskin States'
YEAR RELEASED
2013
ORIGINAL PURPOSE
Basketball
EXTRAS
Lace jewel;
leather lace pouch

PUMA CLYDE x MITA SNEAKERS

MONEY TALKS

Walt 'Clyde' Frazier was a dominant figure on the hardwood courts of the 70s and has been named one of the NBA's fifty greatest players in the history of basketball. Little wonder he acquired his own signature sneaker, the Puma Clyde.

When Tokyo store Mita Sneakers collaborated with Puma, it wanted to honour Clyde's status, as well as comment on the money-oriented society in which we live today. A high-quality, glossy digital print of $1,000 bills with Clyde's face in the place of the President's was plastered all over the upper, lined with a soft black pigskin.

Only 558 pairs were made and released at eighteen select sneaker boutiques worldwide.

SHOE DATA
EDITION
Mita Sneakers
YEAR RELEASED
2007
ORIGINAL PURPOSE
Basketball
EXTRAS
Extra laces

A JOURNEY BACK IN RHYME

Yo! MTV Raps was a 90s hip-hop show hosted by the likes of Dr Dre, Ed Lover and Fab 5 Freddy; in 2006 Puma paid homage to the cult programme, which had been off-air since 1995, using hip-hop favourite the Clyde. The printed upper reflected the show's graphic identity and the *Yo!* logo featured on the tongue, heel and sockliner. The 'Forever Fresh' shoe embodied a combination of music and sneaker history and was accompanied by a CD titled *A Journey Back in Rhyme* and a pack of *Yo! MTV Raps* collectors' cards. Only 225 pairs of this pink version were released in selected stores.

PUMA CLYDE x YO! MTV RAPS

SHOE DATA

EDITION
Yo! MTV Raps
YEAR RELEASED
2006
ORIGINAL PURPOSE
Basketball
EXTRAS
**Trading cards;
'A Journey Back
in Rhyme' CD**

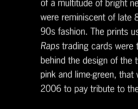

PUMA CLYDE
x YO! MTV RAPS (PROMO)

REPRESENTING THE REAL HIP HOP

The *Yo! MTV Raps* branding consisted of a multitude of bright neon prints that were reminiscent of late 80s and early 90s fashion. The prints used on *Yo! MTV Raps* trading cards were the inspiration behind the design of the two Puma Clydes, pink and lime-green, that were released in 2006 to pay tribute to the show.

The lime-green was a promo edition that came with lime-green laces and, like the pink edition, a CD and collectors' cards. With only fifty pairs made, given away to friends and family and one lucky competition winner, this is a highly sought-after Clyde.

ERIC B. & RAKIM

SHOE DATA

EDITION
Promo
PACK
'Yo! MTV Raps'
YEAR RELEASED
2006
ORIGINAL PURPOSE
Basketball
EXTRAS
**Extra laces;
trading cards;
'A Journey Back
in Rhyme' CD**

83

Artist: TONE LOC
Name: Tony Smith

Yo! Fact: Tone Loc is a former gang member turned rapper from Los Angeles. His positive turn was highlighted when he

PUMA CLYDE x UNDEFEATED 'GAMETIME'

OLYMPIC GOLD

In 2012, as part of an ongoing collaboration, streetwear retailer Undefeated and Puma created a pack of Clydes to be released as the 'Gametime' collection.

The highlight was the metallic '24k' gold Clyde, which honoured the US basketball team for its Gold medal win at the 2012 London Olympics.

This version consisted of a gold perforated-leather upper with red, white and blue dual branding on the tongue label and on the heel pull, an Undefeated lace jewel and a dual-branded leather insole.

These were only available to purchase through Undefeated chapter stores in limited numbers.

SHOE DATA
EDITION
Undefeated
PACK
'Gametime'
YEAR RELEASED
2012
ORIGINAL PURPOSE
Basketball

PUMA CLYDE x UNDEFEATED 'SNAKESKIN'

MAD AS A CUT SNAKE

Rocked by Walt 'Clyde' Frazier on and off the court from 1973 onwards, the Clyde has remained popular for over forty years, with the help of b-boys, streetballers, graffiti artists and worldwide Puma fanatics.

This 'Snakeskin' Clyde pack was the first of many notable releases by Puma and Undefeated in 2012.

The pack consisted of premium-leather Clydes in three classic colourways, accented with a luxe black snakeskin Formstripe and dual-branded woven label on the tongue.

A promo-only version, in a turquoise colourway, was also produced in a limited run of nine pairs. These were available to purchase from the Puma store at the Boxpark pop-up mall in Shoreditch, London.

SHOE DATA

EDITION
Undefeated
PACK
'Snakeskin'
YEAR RELEASED
2012
ORIGINAL PURPOSE
Basketball

181

PUMA SUEDE CLASSIC
x SHINZO 'USAIN BOLT'

SHOE DATA

EDITION
'Usain Bolt'
PACK
'Shinzo'
YEAR RELEASED
2011
ORIGINAL PURPOSE
Basketball
EXTRAS
Dust bag

BOLT OF ECO-THINKING

The relationship between Puma and the current fastest man in the world, Usain Bolt, has been ongoing since Bolt's record-breaking win at the Youth World Championships in 2003, at the age of sixteen.

The year 2011 was a remarkable one for Bolt: he won nine out of the ten races in which he competed, setting new world records and becoming a household name. In honour of his achievements, Puma and Paris retailer Shinzo teamed up to create a limited edition collection dedicated to the Jamaican track star, with a pack consisting of a Puma Suede and two Puma Mids.

Each sneaker was made up of eco-friendly suede with organic cotton canvas lining, a cork insole, recycled foam last and re-ground rubber outsole.

The suede featured details such as the Usain Bolt lion logo on the tongue label, with 'Shinzo' replacing the normal 'Suede' branding, and a painted Formstripe.

Each pair also came with a bespoke dust bag, dual branding and a breakdown of the materials used. The line was sold through Shinzo and select Puma stockists.

PUMA SUEDE CYCLE x MITA SNEAKERS

NIGHT RIDER

In 2013 Japanese boutique Mita Sneakers teamed up with Puma for a collaboration on a new model. The concept for the Puma Suede Cycle, as the name suggests, was based around creating the perfect cycling shoe for navigating the busy streets of Tokyo at night.

LED strobe lights on both heeltabs ensured the wearer could be clearly seen by other road users, and a cover kept the cyclist's laces neatly out the way.

Both the black and brown low-tops maintained the classic lines of the Puma Suede and came in quality leather with gum soles (pictured here are early samples featuring white soles). Mita's signature wire mesh could be found on the insoles together with the Puma logo and the UCI (Union Cycliste Internationale) colours featured on the heel pull.

183

PUMA R698
x CLASSIC KICKS

GOOD THINGS COME
IN THREES

In 2011 Puma worked with New York-based retailer Classic Kicks to collaborate on three versions of the iconic Puma R698. Each version of the shoe featured a neoprene tongue and came with a matching laptop case.

There's a story behind every colourway in the pack. The sea-green version took inspiration from the adidas Race Walk model featured in Neal Heard's 2003 book *Trainers*. It kept the DNA of the original running model, consisting of nubuck, mesh with 3M underneath, and 3M panels on the upper.

The light grey version was based on an old friendship bracelet that one of the Classic Kicks team had as a child, while the final colour of the pack took some inspiration from the United Arrows New Balance 997 and *Sneaker Freaker*'s Blaze of Glory from 2008.

The pack was available from select retailers worldwide, with the sea-green version reportedly limited to 200 shoes.

SHOE DATA

EDITION
The List
PACK
'Classic Kicks'
YEAR RELEASED
2011
ORIGINAL PURPOSE
Running
TECHNOLOGY
Trinomic
EXTRAS
Laptop case

PUMA
x SHADOW SOCIETY

PUMA'S SECRET SOCIETY

In 2011 the Shadow Society, a secret group of Puma connoisseurs, were given control of their own line within Puma to create premium-quality sneaker and apparel collections.

The first collection included three batches of the Puma State, each released shortly after the other. All featured pigskin suede upper and leather lining with laser-etched branding on the back, and came with a leather lace pouch containing spare laces.

The first pack consisted of turquoise and grey colourways; fuchsia and black/green were in the second; and two pairs of Gore-Tex lined States were in the third, one purple and one red.

A year later, the Shadow Society also released two versions of the Trinomic R698 and an updated version of the outdoor 1982 ZDC82 Trainers.

SHOE DATA

EDITION
The List
PACK
'Shadow Society'
YEAR RELEASED
2011/2012
ORIGINAL PURPOSE
Basketball; running
TECHNOLOGY
Trinomic
EXTRAS
Laces in
leather pouch

PUMA DISC BLAZE OG
x RONNIE FIEG

RONNIE REMODELS

In 2012 New Yorker and KITH owner Ronnie Fieg released his first collaboration with Puma, working with the Disc Blaze OG.

The Cove blue colourway – seen on a pair of ASICS Gel-Lyte IIIs that Fieg released in 2010 – was used across the nubuck upper in contrast with a black disc and strapping. The intricate detailing on the shoe included a reflective Formstripe, leather on the vamp and quarter panels, 'RF' branding on the tongue, heel and insole, and KITH's 'Just Us' logo on the leather pull and midsole.

KITH released an individually numbered bespoke box – a first for Puma – featuring custom wrapping paper with sketches of the design process for the first 200 in-store customers, with 100 pairs allocated to each KITH location in Manhattan and Brooklyn. Other regular boxed versions were available to very select retailers worldwide; they sold out instantly.

SHOE DATA

EDITION
Ronnie Fieg
YEAR RELEASED
2012
ORIGINAL PURPOSE
Running
TECHNOLOGY
Trinomic; Disc
EXTRAS
Limited edition bespoke box;
custom wrapping paper

BEAMS CELEBRATE WITH PUMA

As a part of its 35th anniversary, Japanese retailer Beams teamed up with Puma to produce two versions of the Disc Blaze LTWT.

The silhouette was based on a Faas 500 sole unit, with the addition of Disc Blaze technology worked around a seamless mesh upper.

The two editions featured subtle details such as the Beams-branded tongue pull just above the Disc and 'Beams 35' branding on the insole.

PUMA DISC BLAZE LTWT x BEAMS

SHOE DATA

EDITION
Beams
PACK
'35th Anniversary'
YEAR RELEASED
2011
ORIGINAL PURPOSE
Running
TECHNOLOGY
Faas 500 BioRide; EcoOrthoLite; Disc;
KMS Lite; EverTrack; EverRide
EXTRAS
Silk bag; alternate laces

SHOE DATA

EDITION
Sneaker Freaker 'Bunyip'
YEAR RELEASED
2012
ORIGINAL PURPOSE
Basketball
EXTRAS
Extra laces;
print tissue

PUMA DALLAS 'BUNYIP' LO
x SNEAKER FREAKER

188

ABORIGINAL BEAST
COMES TO LIFE

With a concept inspired by the Bunyip, a large mythical creature from Australian Aboriginal mythology, Puma and *Sneaker Freaker* magazine teamed up to turn this beast into a reality, releasing the Bunyip into the world.

Sneaker Freaker made a few modifications to the Puma Dallas model, curbing the performance features and going for a more premium and understated approach; the silhouette featured a goat-suede upper and natural leather lining atop a leather midsole and crêpe sole.

The Dallas branding was changed to 'Bunyip', with *Sneaker Freaker* branding stitched on the reverse of the tongue and mythical branding on the leather insole.

SHOE DATA

EDITION
Hypebeast
PACK
'Dim Sum Project'
YEAR RELEASED
2013
ORIGINAL PURPOSE
Running
TECHNOLOGY
Trinomic; Faas 300
BioRide; ghillie
lacing
EXTRAS
Tote bag

PUMA BLAZE OF GLORY x HYPEBEAST

EAT YOUR HEART OUT: DIM SUM FUN

Hong Kong streetwear blog Hypebeast is a well-known source for trends and progressions in fashion and culture, with a particular focus on sneakers.

Its 'Dim Sum Project' Puma pack was a reflection of its home city and the growing food culture there. Drawing influence from Har Gow and Siu Mai, two dim sum delicacies that are usually ordered together, Hypebeast chose to work on complementary shoes: the original Blaze of Glory, Puma's running silhouette from the early 90s, and the evolved, lightweight Blaze of Glory LTWT.

Siu Mai is a pork-based dumpling with a yellow-hued wrapper; to reflect this on the shoe, a tonal yellow upper made of soft suedes and leathers was used, while the red roe in the dish was depicted along the sole of the sneaker.

Delicate in appearance, Har Gow dumplings have a translucent skin that contains a shrimp-based filling; hence the lightweight dual layers on the Blaze of Glory LTWT and matching colourway.

REEBOK

The history of Reebok has been a long and colourful one. Originally based largely around the sport of running, the firm's story has evolved, along with its sneakers, to encompass much more.

Reebok became the brand most associated with the fitness craze in the 1980s, as well as the leading athletic footwear choice for women, which brought in huge revenues, particularly in the United States. This equipped Reebok with the resources to invest in R&D, which it used to great effect in the 80s and 90s with the introduction of several groundbreaking sneaker technologies including Pump,

Hexalite and DMX, all of which live on to this day. Pump was used on Shaquille O'Neal's first Reebok signature basketball sneaker, and has since spawned endless collaborations with streetwear brands the world over, from Alife (page 198) to Solebox (page 201).

Signing rookie of the year Allen Iverson in 1996 brought about many successful Questions and Answers, two of Reebok's most successful basketball silhouettes. The Question Mid was celebrated ten years after its release by fans Undefeated (page 200). Reebok also displayed a certain degree of prescience with its 2003 decision to sign

rap star Jay-Z to an endorsement line that allowed for his own S. Carter range (which we featured in our first book). Although ultimately unsuccessful, the line was the forerunner of the trend for hip-hop mogul/sportswear crossovers that is still going strong across the industry. Reebok followed on successfully with the Ice Cream range by Pharrell Williams and A Bathing Ape's Nigo (page 197), combining brightly coloured pop culture with high-end appeal. These are just a few of the many collaborators who have reinterpreted the brand's impressive array of sneakers.

SHOE DATA
EDITION
Mita Sneakers
PACK
'30th Anniversary'
YEAR RELEASED
2013
ORIGINAL PURPOSE
Running
TECHNOLOGY
EVA midsole

REEBOK CLASSIC LEATHER x MITA SNEAKERS

30 YEARS OF CLASSIC LEATHER

Introduced in 1983, the Reebok Classic Leather was one of the first sneakers to emphasize casual wear over peak performance. The removable moulded PU foam insole provided extra cushioning while the soft garment leather added both comfort and style.

This 30th anniversary version produced in conjunction with Mita Sneakers in Tokyo used a premium two-tone suede upper in dark blue and contrasting cream, with chambray underlays that featured glow-in-the-dark stars with a soft loopback terry lining.

The Japanese SMU was finished with a gum outsole, while the familiar wire-fence motif and Mita Sneakers branding could be found on the tongue label, lace aglets and sockliner.

REEBOK CLASSIC LEATHER
MID STRAP LUX x KEITH HARING

POSTHUMOUS TRIBUTE TO AN ART LEGEND

New York street-art icon Keith Haring's distinctive style came to life on this sneaker, more than twenty years after his untimely death in 1990. Haring was well known for his bold lines, vivid colours and active figures, all of which were featured on the shoe.

Based on Haring's 'Barking Dogs' artwork, these mid-cuts feature 'Barking Dog' attachments on the Velcro straps, with each foot appearing to bark at the other in mismatched blue and yellow.

The Keith Haring Foundation created a capsule collection based on Haring's artworks, each translated onto different Reebok silhouettes.

SHOE DATA

EDITION
'Barking Dogs'
PACK
'Keith Haring'
YEAR RELEASED
2013
ORIGINAL PURPOSE
Running
TECHNOLOGY
EVA midsole

REEBOK WORKOUT PLUS
'25TH ANNIVERSARY' EDITIONS

25 YEARS IN
THE MAKING

Originally designed as a multi-discipline shoe in 1984, Reebok's Workout was later given a small makeover in 1987 with extra panelling on the forefoot, and called the Workout Plus. For the Workout Plus's 25th anniversary in 2012, Reebok commissioned fifteen retailers to develop a unique shoe using the concept of 'workout'.

Patta deconstructed the concept of exercise, choosing to focus on the speed and agility of a hare, as opposed to that of a tortoise, which led to the furry upper found on the store's interpretation.

Footpatrol's inspiration was its home city of London, specifically the weather and concrete streetscape, but a flash of yellow can be found on the tongue logo – a glimpse of Londoners' hope when the sun occasionally comes out to play.

Mita's choice of materials was all about function, but, as usual, style came to the fore. The strong workwear aesthetic was played up with a hardwearing duck-canvas upper, gum outsole, striped wool lining and hiking bootlaces.

SHOE DATA
PACK
'Workout 25th Anniversary'
YEAR RELEASED
2012
ORIGINAL PURPOSE
Fitness
TECHNOLOGY
Thick moulded sole
EXTRAS
Varsity jacket;
hardcover book

REEBOK INSTA PUMP FURY
x MITA SNEAKERS

FEEL THE FURY

A number of limited edition sneakers have featured prints borrowed from the animal kingdom, one of the most popular being leopard. In 2012 Mita Sneakers used the pattern on the Reebok Insta Pump Fury to great effect.

Originally released in 1993, the Insta Pump Fury was hugely popular due to its technical dominance and head-turning looks, especially in Japan. For this version, although the majority of the upper was covered in leopard print, all of the lightweight synthetic materials usually seen on the model featured grey, black and red accents.

Mita worked on another Insta Pump Fury in conjunction with Hiroshi 'Kirk' Kakiage, designer and founder of the EXPANSION clothing line, who frequently fuses his work with music, art and popular culture in New York and Japan.

Tiger Camouflage, one of Hiroshi's trademark prints, was used on the upper. Other details included Mita branding underneath the tongue pull and 'TYO NYC Reebok Trading' text on Mita's fence graphic insole.

As with the majority of Mita's collaborations, both models were extremely limited and Japan-only releases.

SHOE DATA
EDITION
Mita Sneakers
YEAR RELEASED
2012
ORIGINAL PURPOSE
Running
TECHNOLOGY
**Pump; Hexalite;
3D Ultralite sole**

SHOE DATA

EDITION
CLUCT x Mita Sneakers
YEAR RELEASED
2009
ORIGINAL PURPOSE
Basketball
TECHNOLOGY
EVA midsole

REEBOK EX-O-FIT
x CLUCT x MITA SNEAKERS

TONE AND TEXTURE MAKE FOR A CLASSY SHOE

Since 2008 CLUCT has produced clothing that combines an American flavour with European finesse. In 2009 the brand teamed up with Mita Sneakers and Reebok to create their own version of the then-new release Ex-O-Fit Strap Hi.

Soon after the Ex-O-Fit Strap Hi's inception, several collaborators added their own touches to the model, including Atmos and Mita Sneakers in a solo effort.

For this make-up, the concept was toned down to show that subtlety and considered detailing can be just as effective as a bold and bright design. The mainly black upper features faux croc-skin on the upper heel, a yellow strip dividing the ankle section, 'emphasize, authentic, create and establish' type wrapped around the side panels and script embroidery of the words 'Clutch & Fact' (which together make up the name CLUCT) on the heel, all sitting atop a white sole unit.

REEBOK ICE CREAM LOW
x BILLIONAIRE BOYS CLUB

BATHING IN BILLIONAIRE APPEAL

Originally founded as a collaborative effort between Pharrell Williams and Nigo, founder of A Bathing Ape, the Billionaire Boys Club (BBC) and Ice Cream labels were intended as sister brands to the successful A Bathing Ape venture. While BBC was solely for clothing, the Ice Cream brand also featured a collection of Reebok sneakers. The first model released was called the Ice Cream Low aka Boutique, due to its limited numbers and the fact that it was only available at select boutique stores.

Pharrell's BBC label went on to design the flamboyant version of the Ice Cream pictured here, of which only 170 individually numbered pairs were made and sold exclusively at A Bathing Ape's Busy Workshop store in NYC. It was given a premium feel with silver finished leather, and dollar signs and diamonds were printed on the upper in navy blue. The red, which featured on the outsole and heeltab, provided contrast.

SHOE DATA
EDITION
Billionaire Boys Club
YEAR RELEASED
2005
ORIGINAL PURPOSE
Lifestyle
EXTRAS
Custom box

REEBOK COURT FORCE VICTORY PUMP
x ALIFE 'THE BALL OUT'

LOVE GAME

Following its original green 'Tennis Ball' Court Force Victory Pump collaboration with Reebok in 2006, Alife went on for a second set and created two more colourways later that year.

The new release consisted of orange and white versions, both using the same tennis-ball felt on the upper. The limited availability of the two designs ensured that they quickly sold out, and they both remain highly sought after.

A year later Alife released two additional colours – pink and black – that saw a slightly wider distribution; previous versions had been exclusive to Alife locations.

SHOE DATA
EDITION
Alife
PACK
'The Ball Out'
YEAR RELEASED
2006
ORIGINAL PURPOSE
Tennis
TECHNOLOGY
Pump
EXTRAS
Extra laces

SHOE DATA

EDITION
Deadpool
PACK
'Marvel'
YEAR RELEASED
2012
ORIGINAL PURPOSE
Basketball
TECHNOLOGY
Pump; Hexalite

199

COMIC BOOK KICKS ASS

In 2012, following the popular releases of its Captain America and Wolverine collaborations with Reebok, Marvel unleashed the Reebok Pump Omni Lite Deadpool, inspired by the X-Force mercenary comic book character.

The strong black/red colourway echoed that of Deadpool's costume, while two Adamantium swords – his weapon of choice – were found crossed on the heel. Other detailing included red, black and grey branding, not to mention a ferociously posed Deadpool image split across the two insoles.

REEBOK PUMP OMNI LITE
x 'MARVEL' DEADPOOL

QUESTIONS TO PONDER

Reebok signed basketball player Allen Iverson to a ten-year contract in 1996, his rookie year, and his signature shoe, the Question, went on to become one of Reebok's best-selling models of all time.

The year 2006 marked the 10th anniversary of the signing, and to celebrate this, Undefeated developed its own multicoloured version, featuring giant 'IVERSON' lettering next to the lace loops, '96' on the heel panel and a black-speckled orange Hexalite sole unit.

For the launch, Undefeated in Los Angeles placed winning tickets inside the boxes of three pairs. One lucky person would win a pair of sneakers signed by Allen Iverson, another a signed hat and the third a signed basketball.

SHOE DATA

EDITION
Undefeated
YEAR RELEASED
2006
ORIGINAL PURPOSE
Basketball
TECHNOLOGY
**Hexalite; ghillie
lacing**

REEBOK PUMP OMNI ZONE LT x SOLEBOX

LIGHTING UP THE COURT

In 2011 Berlin-based trainer boutique Solebox released its latest collaboration with Reebok: the Pump Omni Zone LT.

The modern take had orange LED lights on the outer side panel of each foot, which could be illuminated with the push of a button that was subtly tucked away on the tongue. Further features included a battery pack in a small pouch just underneath the size label, 3M detailing on the tongue and Solebox branding on the insole.

As the first release sold so well, in 2012 Solebox created a second version to coincide with its 10th anniversary, this time using green LED lights. Each pair came with a free matching glow-in-the-dark tote bag.

Limited to 100 pairs, both colours were exclusively sold in-store and online from Solebox.

SHOE DATA

EDITION
Solebox
YEAR RELEASED
2011
ORIGINAL PURPOSE
Basketball
TECHNOLOGY
ERS; Pump; LED light
EXTRAS
Glow-in-the-dark tote bag;
Pump swing tag

VANS

Vans has one of the most storied histories of any footwear brand. From its humble beginnings as a small, passionate family firm in 1960s California, to its place today as one of the world's biggest and most influential action sports companies, it provides a great example of the potential of the American dream to go global.

The brand encompasses the worlds of skate, surf, BMX, snow and a host of other extreme sports, but it is perhaps in the sphere of music that Vans holds the most sway. Effortlessly ingratiating itself across a range of musical subcultures, Vans is the first sneaker brand with which many die-hard music fans will immediately associate themselves. Collaborations with stadium-filling bands such as Metallica and Iron Maiden, alongside bespoke efforts for more niche bands – think the Bad Brains collection (pages 216–17) or working with Lupe

Fiasco as part of the OTW lifestyle collection – mean that Vans can truly say it represents cultures across the whole spectrum of modern music.

Vans has also spread across a wide range of popular cultures with its easy-to-wear and easy-on-the-eye silhouettes that have served as a perfect blank canvas for many artistically inclined collaborators. From *The Simpsons* (pages 208–9) to streetwear store Supreme (no less than five Supreme sneakers appear in the following pages), Vans has, arguably more than any other brand, been able to reach out and touch a huge number of consumers with its collaborations.

The brand has dipped into the world of high fashion through its ongoing collection with legendary American designer Marc Jacobs (page 204), and has also offered up some of its most recognizable silhouettes for reworking by the likes of West Coast tattoo legend Mr Cartoon (page 219) and Japanese cult brand WTAPS (page 220).

This diversity of collaborative products sums up Vans – it's the footwear brand that seems to have something for everybody.

VANS CLASSIC SLIP-ON LUX
x MARC JACOBS

CATWALK MEETS SIDEWALK

Vans first partnered with high-end fashion label Marc Jacobs in spring 2005, attracting the attention of sneakerheads and fashionistas alike.

Marc Jacobs worked on an assortment of different models but applied the most experimental designs to the Classic Slip-on.

This particular edition drew inspiration from television test patterns, which indicated the transmitter was active but no programme was being broadcast.

The line was a huge success and the limited release quickly sold out.

VANS CLASSIC SLIP-ON
x CLOT

TRIBESMEN ON HOLIDAY

In 2012 Vans teamed up for the first time with Hong Kong-based streetwear brand CLOT to release a holiday collection.

The inspiration came from CLOT's autumn/winter 2012 collection, 'Tribesmen', and made use of embroidery and bright colouring on four Vans Era and Classic Slip-On models.

The Eras featured a washed-out canvas upper with matching tonal midsole, stand-out white laces and 'Tribesmen' detailing on the tongue and heel.

The Classic Slip-On (featured here) gave a much more overt shout-out to the 'Tribesmen' influence, with the bright woven pattern covering the front of the shoe as well as the heel, contrasting with the plain midsole.

The collection was released exclusively a week early at CLOT's designer streetwear store, JUICE, in Hong Kong. Regional releases followed as the collection was made available across Asia at other JUICE stores.

SHOE DATA

EDITION
CLOT
YEAR RELEASED
2012
ORIGINAL PURPOSE
Skateboarding
TECHNOLOGY
**Vulcanized sole;
waffle sole**

VANS SYNDICATE x **WTAPS**

PENTAGRAMS AND BONES

Premium Japanese streetwear label WTAPS is heavily influenced by skate, punk, military and motorcycle aesthetics, and this was strongly reflected throughout its first Vans Syndicate collaboration, entitled 'Bones and Wings'.

The autumn 2006 collection consisted of four Vans Syndicate models: the Sk8-Hi, Chukka and Slip-On came under the first 'Bones' release, while the 'Wings' dropped later and contained three versions of the Authentic. The three 'Bones' models featured an all-over crossbones print, while the Slip-On highlighted a Slayer-style pentagram on the foxing and around the shoe's collar.

Shown here are early samples that were never released (featuring the pentagram prominently across all three silhouettes), and the publicly released Slip-On (in the centre).

SHOE DATA
EDITION
WTAPS
PACK
'Bones'
YEAR RELEASED
2006
ORIGINAL PURPOSE
Skateboarding
TECHNOLOGY
Vulcanized sole;
waffle sole
EXTRAS
Syndicate box;
leather hang tag;
Syndicate sticker

VANS x THE SIMPSONS

DO THE BARTMAN, ART STYLE

The long-awaited *Simpsons Movie* was finally released in July 2007. To commemorate the occasion, Vans got together with twelve different artists, each of whom worked on a silhouette from a choice of classic models including the Sk8-Hi and -Mid, Chukka Boot, Era and Slip-On.

The artist roster included luminaries such as KAWS, Stash, Mr Cartoon, Futura and Neckface to name a few – a tribute to the cartoon family's enduring influence throughout many subcultures.

Each unique sneaker was representative of the artist's individual style, and each artist was also portrayed as a Matt Groening caricature on a specially made slide-out drawer box.

Only 100 pairs of each style were produced and distributed among ten stores in the US. The complete collection sold out instantly and the shoes are now highly valued collectors' items.

SHOE DATA

EDITION
The Simpsons
PACK
'The Simpsons Movie'
YEAR RELEASED
2007
ORIGINAL PURPOSE
Skateboarding
TECHNOLOGY
Vulcanized sole;
waffle sole
EXTRAS
Custom box

Left to right

Chukka Boot LX x Geoff McFetridge
Slip-On LX x Sam Messer
Chukka Boot LX x Neckface
Slip-On LX x Tony Munoz
Chukka Boot LX x KAWS
Sk8-Mid LX x Futura
Era LX x Gary Panter
Sk8-Hi LX x Taka Hayashi
Slip-On LX x Mr Cartoon
Slip-On LX x David Flores
Sk8-Mid LX x Stash
Sk8-Hi LX x Todd James (REAS)

VANS x KENZO

THE CALIFORNIA CONNECTION

After breathing new life into Parisian fashion house Kenzo in 2012, the creative directors of the brand, Humberto Leon and Carol Lim (of Opening Ceremony fame), teamed up with Vans.

With separate releases staggered month by month, Kenzo applied designs from its collection to the uppers, starting off with a fishnet pattern, then using floral and striped prints for the second collection, and monochrome moth, striped and marbled prints for the third.

The third was the first to feature the Slip-On, while the previous two had included only the Authentic.

The collection was made in limited numbers and only distributed to select retail partners, including Opening Ceremony, Selfridges, Liberty, Colette and I.T in Hong Kong.

SHOE DATA

EDITION
Kenzo
YEAR RELEASED
2012
ORIGINAL PURPOSE
Skateboarding
TECHNOLOGY
Vulcanized sole;
waffle sole

VANS AUTHENTIC PRO x SUPREME
x COMME DES GARÇONS SHIRT

THEY MEAN BUSINESS

Dover Street Market (DSM), the London flagship boutique of Japanese fashion label Comme des Garçons, houses a broad range of brands, from streetwear to high-end clothing.

Supreme was one of the labels stocked at DSM, so a collaboration between the two brands made sense. For spring/summer 2013 they released a clothing collection containing button-down shirts, camp caps, pullover hoodies and tees.

Following on from the clothing collection, Supreme also worked with Vans on new versions of the Authentic and Sk8-Hi models.

Both models featured a preppy blue-and-white pinstriped upper with embossed branding on the insole.

This collection was only available through DSM, Supreme retail spaces and the Comme des Garçons I.T Beijing Market.

SHOE DATA

EDITION
Supreme x Comme
des Garçons SHIRT
YEAR RELEASED
2012
ORIGINAL PURPOSE
Skateboarding
TECHNOLOGY
Vulcanized sole;
waffle sole

211

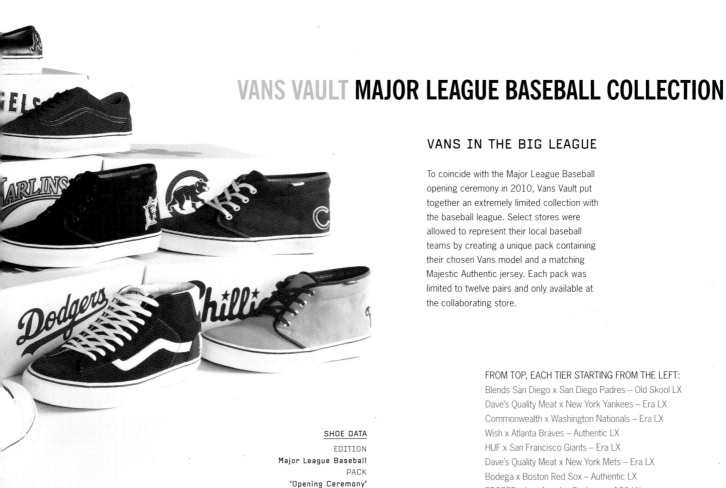

VANS VAULT **MAJOR LEAGUE BASEBALL COLLECTION**

VANS IN THE BIG LEAGUE

To coincide with the Major League Baseball opening ceremony in 2010, Vans Vault put together an extremely limited collection with the baseball league. Select stores were allowed to represent their local baseball teams by creating a unique pack containing their chosen Vans model and a matching Majestic Authentic jersey. Each pack was limited to twelve pairs and only available at the collaborating store.

SHOE DATA
EDITION
Major League Baseball
PACK
'Opening Ceremony'
YEAR RELEASED
2010
ORIGINAL PURPOSE
Skateboarding
TECHNOLOGY
Vulcanized sole;
waffle sole
EXTRAS
Custom box; Majestic
Authentic jersey

FROM TOP, EACH TIER STARTING FROM THE LEFT:
Blends San Diego x San Diego Padres – Old Skool LX
Dave's Quality Meat x New York Yankees – Era LX
Commonwealth x Washington Nationals – Era LX
Wish x Atlanta Braves – Authentic LX
HUF x San Francisco Giants – Era LX
Dave's Quality Meat x New York Mets – Era LX
Bodega x Boston Red Sox – Authentic LX
PROPER x Los Angeles Dodgers – 106 LX
Blends x Los Angeles Angels Of Anaheim – Old Skool LX
Saint Alfred x Chicago White Sox – Chukka LX
Bows & Arrows x Oakland Athletics – Chukka LX
C'MON x Baltimore Orioles – Sk8-Hi LX
Shoe Gallery x Florida Marlins – Chukka LX
Saint Alfred x Chicago Cubs – Chukka LX
Conveyer at Fred Segal x Los Angeles Dodgers – Sk8-Hi LX
PROPER x Los Angeles Angels Of Anaheim – Chukka LX
Undefeated x Los Angeles Dodgers – Old Skool LX
Ubiq x Philadelphia Phillies – Chukka LX

VANS AUTHENTIC PRO & HALF CAB PRO
x SUPREME 'CAMPBELL'S SOUP'

TWO ICONIC MOTIFS UNITE

In 2012 New York-based skate-turned-streetwear impresarios Supreme looked to Andy Warhol's classic 'Campbell's Soup' Pop-art motif for inspiration on this bold collaboration with Vans.

The famous design is instantly recognizable on all three silhouettes, with an all-over print on the Authentic and Half Cab (shown here), and the side panel print contrasting against black on the Sk8-Hi. The choice of this motif, with its use of white lettering on red, also gives a nod to Supreme's own iconic boxed logo.

The collection was initially released in Japan, with later drops at Supreme stores in New York, Los Angeles and London, as well as online. 'Campbell's Soup' all-over print T-shirts and mesh caps were also available alongside the sneaker release.

SHOE DATA

EDITION
Supreme
YEAR RELEASED
2012
ORIGINAL PURPOSE
Skateboarding
TECHNOLOGY
Vulcanized sole;
waffle sole
EXTRAS
Extra laces (black);
Campbell's Soup T-shirt

VANS ERA x COLETTE x COBRASNAKE

GOT BEEF?

In 2012 renowned Los Angeles-based street fashion photographer Mark Hunter, aka The Cobrasnake, teamed up with French boutique Colette to create a unique take on the Vans Era.

Ten years before the release of the shoe, Hunter had been an avid burger eater; he eventually changed his ways and became a vegetarian. The Cobrasnake Era pays homage to his former love of burgers.

The illustrated 6 oz canvas upper breaks down the staple ingredients found in an American hamburger, from the seeded bun down to the cheese and meat.

Only sixty pairs were made, and were available exclusively from the Colette store in Paris.

SHOE DATA

EDITION
Colette x Cobrasnake
YEAR RELEASED
2012
ORIGINAL PURPOSE
Skateboarding
TECHNOLOGY
Vulcanized sole;
waffle sole

THE COBRA SNAKE
t food for your feet
colette:

VANS SK8-HI x SUPREME x BAD BRAINS

SKATE MEETS PUNK

The cultures of skateboarding and punk music have always had a close affiliation; it is an understanding that skate-turned-streetwear brand Supreme and seminal punk and hardcore band Bad Brains encapsulated in their 2008 collection for Vans.

The collaboration focused on the three Rastafarian colours of red, gold and green, with a shoe devoted to each.

'Coptic Times', the name of the first track on Bad Brains' *Rock For Light* LP, was written across the heel counters. Supreme also released two T-shirts and a Harrington jacket as part of the collection.

Vans followed up with its own separate Bad Brains and Supreme collections.

SHOE DATA

EDITION
Supreme x Bad Brains
YEAR RELEASED
2008
ORIGINAL PURPOSE
Skateboarding
TECHNOLOGY
Vulcanized sole;
waffle sole

VANS x BAD BRAINS

RASTA ROCK STYLES

Vans teamed up with Bad Brains again in spring 2009, this time to produce versions of the Sk8-Hi, Chukka and 46 LE.

The pack was tied together with artwork on the premium slide-out drawer box and tote bag.

A clothing collection of branded T-shirts, board shorts, belts and wallets was later released in spring 2010.

The collection featured Bad Brains' Rastafarian-inspired album artwork, taken from their first full-length studio album, *Bad Brains*, and their 2007 release, *Build a Nation*.

SHOE DATA
EDITION
Bad Brains
YEAR RELEASED
2009
ORIGINAL PURPOSE
Skateboarding
TECHNOLOGY
Vulcanized sole;
waffle sole
EXTRAS
Custom box; tote bag

VANS SK8 x SUPREME
'PUBLIC ENEMY'

SHOE DATA

EDITION
Supreme
PACK
'Public Enemy'
YEAR RELEASED
2006
ORIGINAL PURPOSE
Skateboarding
TECHNOLOGY
Vulcanized sole;
waffle sole
EXTRAS
Extra laces

FUELLING A MOVEMENT THROUGH MUSIC

Chuck D, Flavor Flav, Professor Griff and Terminator X, also known as Public Enemy, have been expressing their political views through hip-hop from 1982 to the present day.

When skate- and streetwear stalwart Supreme started its seventh footwear collaboration with Vans, it took its fellow New Yorkers as inspiration, placing the inimitable Public Enemy cross-hair logo on the sides of two Sk8-His over classic Vans colourways from the mid-90s.

It Takes a Nation of Millions to Hold Us Back, the title of Public Enemy's second album in 1988, was printed across the midsoles of both. T-shirts, hoodies and beanies were also released as part of the collection.

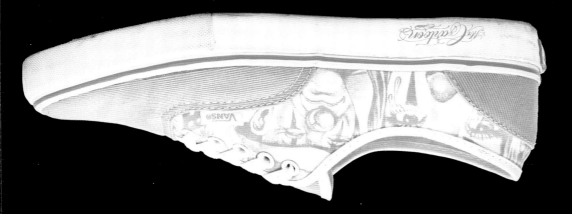

SHOE DATA

EDITION
Syndicate
PACK
'Mr Cartoon'
YEAR RELEASED
2005
ORIGINAL PURPOSE
Skateboarding
TECHNOLOGY
Vulcanized sole;
waffle sole

VANS AUTHENTIC SYNDICATE x MR CARTOON

CLOWNING AROUND

Mr Cartoon is a tattoo and graffiti artist who hails from Los Angeles. With a client list that reads like a who's who of the hip-hop industry, and a range of sneaker collaborations to date, he has become an acclaimed figure in both footwear and tattoo circles.

For his first project with Vans, also part of the very first Syndicate range, Mr Cartoon worked with the Authentic;

the suitably clean upper of the silhouette allowed him to express his creativity with ease.

The pack contained three colourways, all of which featured a canvas-and-denim upper, clown artwork on the side panels and Mr Cartoon's famous angel design on the insole.

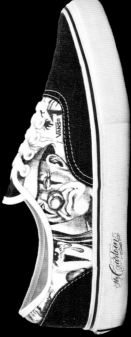

VANS SYNDICATE
x WTAPS NO GUTS NO GLORY SK8-HI

SHOE DATA
EDITION
Syndicate
PACK
'WTAPS'
YEAR RELEASED
2007
ORIGINAL PURPOSE
Skateboarding
TECHNOLOGY
Vulcanized sole;
waffle sole

A GUTSY APPROACH
FROM WTAPS

This 2007 Syndicate release wasn't Vans' first collaboration with Japanese streetwear company WTAPS, but it was definitely the boldest to date. Three versions of the Vans Sk8-Hi were made up to coincide with WTAPS' spring/summer collection entitled 'No Guts No Glory'.

A black suede toe box complemented the busy printed canvas emblazoned with 'No Guts No Glory' on the panelling. Each shoe also had a small logo printed on the outsole. Available in white, green and orange versions, this premium take on the popular skate shoe was only available at select Syndicate retailers.

VANS SK8-HI & ERA
x SUPREME
x ARI MARCOPOULOS

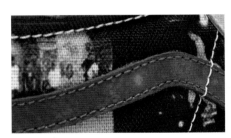

DOCUMENTING SKATE LEGACY

Amsterdam-born photographer and filmmaker Ari Marcopoulos moved to New York City in 1979, where he worked with Andy Warhol and photographed numerous artists and musicians, including the Beastie Boys. In 1994 the Supreme store opened; Ari was a regular face there, documenting the skaters that Supreme was supporting, and immersing himself in the culture.

In 2006 he teamed up with Supreme to create a clothing collection that included a hooded sweatshirt and a five-panel cap; the two also worked with Vans to design a footwear collection featuring three Eras and three Sk8-His. Each had a printed canvas upper featuring images of skateboarders photographed by Ari.

Both collections were exclusively sold at Supreme's New York and LA locations and are now extremely collectable.

SHOE DATA

EDITION
Ari Marcopoulos
PACK
'Supreme'
YEAR RELEASED
2006
ORIGINAL PURPOSE
Skateboarding
TECHNOLOGY
Vulcanized sole;
waffle sole

VANS SYNDICATE CHUKKA LO
x CIVILIST

SHOE DATA

EDITION
Civilist
YEAR RELEASED
2011
ORIGINAL PURPOSE
Skateboarding
TECHNOLOGY
Bellows; Dri-Lex; vulcanized
sole; waffle sole
EXTRAS
Cufflinks; T-shirt;
tote bag

CIVILIZED SKATEWEAR

In 2011 Vans Syndicate teamed up with Berlin skate shop Civilist to produce a subtle, premium version of the Chukka Lo. Both Civilist founders had grown up in post-war Berlin, during which time the city was occupied by Allied soldiers. The Chukka Lo was chosen in a nod to the city's troubled history, as British soldiers had worn chukkas during the war.

For inspiration, Civilist went through the Syndicate archives, and chose materials including the absorbent Dri-Lex lining that had been used in the 2008 Gabe Morford Syndicate collection. Further features included bellows (a gusseted tongue) to prevent water entry, copper eyelets (matching the Civilist store fixtures) and a felt Civilist-branded tongue patch (a reference to the city's political past: *Felt* is a term for corruption in German).

Civilist kept the majority of the ninety-eight pairs that were produced, but distributed small numbers to select stores.

SHOE DATA

EDITION
Alakazam
YEAR RELEASED
2012
ORIGINAL PURPOSE
Skateboarding
TECHNOLOGY
Vulcanized sole;
waffle sole

VANS ERA x ALAKAZAM x STÜSSY

OPERATION RADICATION

London-based creative collective Alakazam teamed up with streetwear pioneer Stüssy to create a capsule collection known as 'Operation Radication', with reggae and dub music as the inspiration behind the designs. Alakazam produces T-shirts, prints and books, as well as creating cover art for various musicians and DJs around the world.

This pair of Eras was made from a black denim upper with Rastafarian-coloured eyelets and print on the midsole, and Alakazam founder Will Sweeney's lion logo on the tongue. They were only available to purchase from Stüssy stores in Japan, and Zozotown, the Japanese online retailer, while the apparel collection was distributed through Alakazam's and Stüssy's online stores.

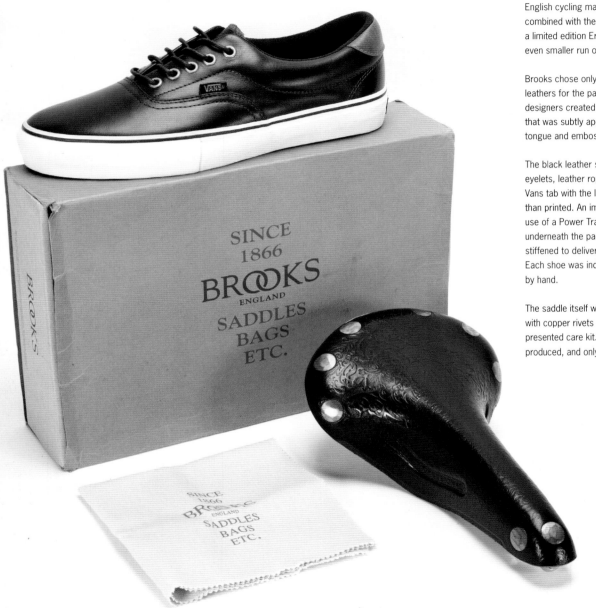

VANS VAULT ERA LX x **BROOKS**

CALI-COOL WITH AN ENGLISH TOUCH

In 2010 the distinctive classic styling of English cycling manufacturer Brooks was combined with the Vans Vault to create a limited edition Era LX, along with an even smaller run of matching saddles.

Brooks chose only the finest saddle leathers for the pack, while Vans designers created a skull-and-flower motif that was subtly applied to the sneaker's tongue and embossed on the saddle.

The black leather shoe featured copper eyelets, leather rope laces and a leather Vans tab with the logo embossed, rather than printed. An improved sole unit made use of a Power Transfer plate that lay underneath the padded insole, which was stiffened to deliver firmer performance. Each shoe was individually numbered by hand.

The saddle itself was also finely finished with copper rivets and a beautifully presented care kit. Some 2,000 pairs were produced, and only 500 of the saddle set.

SHOE DATA

EDITION
Brooks England
YEAR RELEASED
2010
ORIGINAL PURPOSE
Skateboarding
TECHNOLOGY
Power Transfer sole unit; vulcanized sole; waffle sole
EXTRAS
Leather laces; custom box; saddle with care kit: wrench, cloth and leather conditioner

x SUPREME x STEVE CABALLERO

CABALLERO HALVES HIS CABS

Even if you're not into skateboarding or the culture that surrounds it, there's still a good chance that you have heard of the legend that is Steve Caballero.

Vans signed him in 1988 and produced his first signature shoe, the 'Caballero' high-top, a year later.

Over the years, Caballero noticed that skaters would often cut his shoes down to a mid-cut, so in 1992 he passed this information on to Vans, who then created the Half Cab that same year.

To celebrate the Half Cab's 20th anniversary in 2012, Vans released one limited edition version every month over the course of the year.

The first paid tribute to the shoe that started it all, with twenty individually numbered Half Cabs hand-cut, duct-taped and signed by Caballero himself.

The shoe was also produced in collaboration with Supreme, so five pairs made their way to its LA, London, New York and Harajuku stores.

SHOE DATA

EDITION
Supreme x Steve Caballero
PACK
'20th Anniversary'
YEAR RELEASED
2012
ORIGINAL PURPOSE
Skateboarding
TECHNOLOGY
**Vulcanized sole;
waffle sole**
EXTRAS
Signed box

AND NOT FORGETTING

Outside of the sneaker industry's core of big brands, there exists a plethora of smaller companies that produce athletic footwear in competition with the more established players. They often have significant cultural clout and attract a large number of fans and followers. The more memorable limited edition output of several of these smaller brands is outlined in the following pages.

A Bathing Ape (BAPE) is the cult Japanese brand founded by streetwear impresario Nigo in 1993. Originally the line consisted of limited edition apparel, but it was later expanded to include lifestyle footwear, most famously the controversial BAPESTA, which paid overt homage to the Nike Air Force 1 silhouette.

The BAPESTA has been a popular model for collaborations since its inception.

PONY is a brand that has moved beyond the basketball court to create a lifestyle range with a loyal following. It has often been seen as a somewhat New York-centric brand, but many people don't know that PONY stands for Product of New York. This NYC heritage is reflected in the firm's work with Big Apple personalities such as photographer Ricky Powell and fashion designers Dee & Ricky.

PRO-Keds, established by Keds in 1949, also from New York, has a strong basketball heritage with an increasingly influential lifestyle division. Its classic model, the Royal, is a silhouette that is

still a favourite for collaborations due to its clean upper.

Saucony is an athletic footwear company with a rich history in the US that focuses largely on racing, running and walking models. It has also experienced a revival due to the brand's willingness to work on a range of lifestyle sneakers for both limited edition and collaborative projects.

The Lacoste legend was born in 1933 in France. The brand initially focused on producing its now-famous tennis shirt, featuring the oft-copied crocodile logo. But its rich heritage and association with many different subcultures throughout its history have ensured that even today Lacoste remains a popular choice

for collaborators. The company's forays into athletic footwear have generally been well received.

France has a strong tradition of manufacturing sporting goods, a further example being Le Coq Sportif. Originally founded in 1882, this brand has a deep football heritage that remains part of its identity today.

Rounding out the European trifecta of brands is FILA, which also has a rich pedigree, dating back to Italy circa 1911. With a focus on athletic shoes and apparel, FILA has also been strongly represented in a range of collaborative efforts in recent years.

LACOSTE MISSOURI x KIDROBOT

GAME, SET AND MATCH

The 2007 Kidrobot collection for Lacoste comprised three models: the Missouri, Revan 2 and Revan 3. Each had a mix of premium materials on the upper along with graphics inspired by Kidrobot's toy and apparel lines.

The Missouri was given a predominantly grey suede and 3M upper, with a white perforated leather toe box and Kidrobot's 'Bones' graphic on the tongue and the heel panel. The 'Bones' could also be seen on Kidrobot's clothing line from the same season, as well as on some of its Labbit toys.

Kidrobot founders Paul Budnitz and Chad Phillips wanted to cater to the collector's market, limiting each version to 500 pairs worldwide and including a matching PEECOL figure; if you look closely you can see a tennis ball in the PEECOL's pocket.

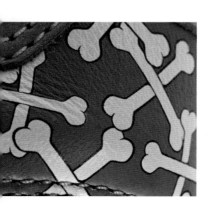

SHOE DATA

EDITION
Kidrobot
YEAR RELEASED
2007
ORIGINAL PURPOSE
Tennis
TECHNOLOGY
Pivot point;
forefoot strap
EXTRAS
'PEECOL' figure

LE COQ SPORTIF ÉCLAT x FOOTPATROL

SHOE DATA
EDITION
Footpatrol
YEAR RELEASED
2012
ORIGINAL PURPOSE
Running
TECHNOLOGY
Plastic heel counter;
gum outsole;
ghillie lacing
EXTRAS
Co-branded socks;
nylon shoe bag;
canvas tote bag

RETRO RUNNING:
FOREVER CLASSIC

Le Coq Sportif's 2012 edition of retro running silhouette the Éclat was the result of its first ever collaboration with London-based sneaker store Footpatrol.

The muted colourway with red accent was based around the idea that the sneaker would be worn year-round. Premium suede, ultra-light nylon and Scotchlite were combined with a rubber gum sole, while the tongue displayed a mash-up of both brands' logos: the Le Coq Sportif triangle was flipped horizontally, with Footpatrol's gas mask logo placed inside.

Only eighty-five pairs were produced to reflect the year in which the model was first released.

229

A BATHING APE BAPESTA
x MARVEL COMICS

SUPER SMASHING BAPE

In 2005 A Bathing Ape (BAPE) and
comic giant Marvel joined forces to
create the Marvel BAPESTAs. The
collection included colourways inspired
by superhero characters such as
Spiderman, Captain America, the
Incredible Hulk, the Silver Surfer,
Thor, Iron Man and the Human Torch.

From the Marvel embroidery, printed
insoles and character decals on the
heels, to the well-thought-out colourways
in line with BAPE's usual standout colour
combos, the attention to detail on the
sneakers is considerable.

All of the Marvel models were produced
in limited edition blister packaging, in a
nod to collectable action toys.

This Incredible Hulk version takes on the
Hulk's signature green 'angry' skin and
ripped purple shorts. Marvel editions
can now fetch up to $450.

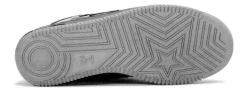

SHOE DATA

EDITION
Incredible Hulk
PACK
'Marvel Comics'
YEAR RELEASED
2005
ORIGINAL PURPOSE
Lifestyle
EXTRAS
Blister pack

A BATHING APE BAPESTA
x NEIGHBORHOOD

SHOE DATA
EDITION
Neighborhood
YEAR RELEASED
2004
ORIGINAL PURPOSE
Lifestyle

A JAPANESE RARITY

Released in 2004, this early collaboration between Japanese streetwear giant A Bathing Ape and Neighborhood was limited to just 100 pairs worldwide.

Many referred to the sneakers as 'Yin Yangs' due to the way the black/white colourway was reversed on the left and right feet. The upper was made from premium leather and finished off with 'NY' embroidered on the heel.

SAUCONY SHADOW 5000
x BODEGA 'ELITE'

CLASSIC MODELS GET
THE CREDIT THEY DESERVE

Saucony and Boston's Bodega teamed up in 2010 to create a new sub-line called Saucony Elite. Aiming to revive classic and underrated models that they believed deserved more recognition, the two companies worked with a mix of premium materials, such as pigskin lining and perforated nubuck, accented with vibrant colours to bring some life back into forgotten sneakers.

One of the shoes in the series was the Shadow 5000, which was originally sold exclusively in the Japanese market. Saucony then decided to let some of its favourite retailers stock it, with a different tongue label – the Japan edition sported a Shadow 5000 label and the worldwide version had a Saucony Elite 'winged' label.

Other models in the line included the Shadow 6000, Hangtime, Elite Grid 9000, Elite Jazz and Master Control.

SHOE DATA

EDITION
Bodega 'Elite'
YEAR RELEASED
2010
ORIGINAL PURPOSE
Running
TECHNOLOGY
Cushioned heel and
ankle collar;
cushioned foot bed;
XT600 rubber outsole;
EVA midsole

FILA TRAILBLAZER
x FOOTPATROL

CLEARING A NEW PATH FOR THE TRAILBLAZER

As one of the standout models from the FILA Mountain collection in the 90s, the Trailblazer was historically popular in the street and UK rave scenes.

In 2012 Footpatrol collaborated with FILA to bring back the Trailblazer and a hybrid called the Trailblazer AM.

Footpatrol's Trailblazer stayed as close to the original as possible, with subtle added details such as a debossed Footpatrol logo on the ankle and dual branding on the insole. The Trailblazer AM was an updated version with new features including a blown rubber outsole, tan leather beading and a smooth premium-nubuck upper.

Two colours of each model made up the pack.

SHOE DATA

EDITION
Footpatrol
YEAR RELEASED
2012
ORIGINAL PURPOSE
Outdoor
TECHNOLOGY
Ghillie lacing; blown rubber outsole

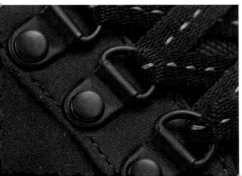

WINTER KICKS WORTH FIGHTING FOR

PRO-Keds collaborated on this limited edition release with heritage outdoor clothing company Woolrich.

Woolrich's famous hunting plaid fabric was used on the upper of the Royal Master DK – an updated version of the original 1972 Royal Master, with the DK's padded ankle support and more refined details applied throughout.

The model was available in three colourways – charcoal, navy and red – with contrast white laces and a rubber toe cap on top of a white vulcanized sole unit. The sneaker displayed PRO-Keds branding on the tongue, as well as signature red and blue power stripes on the white midsole.

PRO-KEDS ROYAL MASTER DK
'HUNTING PLAID' x WOOLRICH

SHOE DATA

EDITION
Woolrich 'Hunting Plaid'
YEAR RELEASED
2012
ORIGINAL PURPOSE
Basketball
TECHNOLOGY
Vulcanized rubber sole; moulded removable foot bed; toe guard

SHOE DATA

EDITION
Patta
PACK
'5th Anniversary'
YEAR RELEASED
2009
ORIGINAL PURPOSE
Basketball
TECHNOLOGY
**Vulcanized sole;
moulded removable
foot bed; toe guard**
EXTRAS
Grocery bag

PRO-KEDS ROYAL LO x **PATTA**

PREMIUM LEATHERS FIT FOR PRO ROYALTY

The year 2009 marked Patta's 5th anniversary, and as part of the celebrations, the Dutch sneaker retailer teamed up with American brand PRO-Keds, which is renowned for its basketball trainers that adorned many players' feet throughout the 70s. For this collaboration, they created premium versions of the Royal Lo and Hi.

The shoes had a white premium pebbled-leather upper with tonal branding, enamel eyelets and leather laces, on top of a classic gum sole. Well known for adding accessories to its releases, Patta also included a heavy-duty canvas-and-leather grocery bag.

PRO-Keds BIZ

PRO-KEDS 69ER LO
x BIZ MARKIE

DEFINITELY DIDN'T SINK

In 2011 PRO-Keds got together with Marcel Hall, aka hip-hop artist Biz Markie, for this version of the 69er Lo sneaker.

Two leather colourways – olive and black, limited to 300 pairs each – were made, with an exclusive white edition produced with retailer Packer Shoes (limited to 150 pairs). All featured a Biz Markie stamp on the tongue and special insoles.

The sneakers came in a premium box with a Biz Markie USB stick.

SHOE DATA
EDITION
Biz Markie
YEAR RELEASED
2011
ORIGINAL PURPOSE
Basketball
TECHNOLOGY
Vulcanized sole; moulded removable foot bed; toe guard
EXTRAS
Premium box; USB stick

PONY SLAM DUNK VINTAGE x RICKY POWELL

SLAM DUNK THE PHOTO FUNK

In 2012 renowned street photographer Ricky Powell, known for his photographs of Def Jam artists such as the Beastie Boys, LL Cool J and Run-DMC, collaborated with Pony on its 1982 basketball model, the Slam Dunk.

As a strict vegetarian, Powell didn't want any animal materials incorporated into the design. Instead, he used a heavily waxed canvas upper to ensure that it would be just as rugged and hardwearing as a leather shoe.

To promote the collaboration, Powell travelled to Footpatrol in London and Amsterdam's SPRMRKT where the collection, including two T-shirts, was showcased at an in-store event alongside a private slide show of Powell's images. Powell signed prints of his famous 'The Dog Walker' photo at the event. His signature could be found on the tongues of the sneakers, and on 'The Dog Walker' image featured on the insoles and lid of the box.

The red/silver vintage Dunk was only released in the US and Japan, whereas the navy/silver version saw a wider release and was given to select Pony accounts.

SHOE DATA

EDITION
Ricky Powell
YEAR RELEASED
2012
ORIGINAL PURPOSE
Basketball
TECHNOLOGY
Vulcanized sole;
toe guard

PONY M100 x DEE & RICKY

TWIN TREADS

Pony recently reissued a 1:1 comeback of the M100, which had first been released in 1988. The model was very high-tech at the time, featuring a breathable moulded side grill, a fast lacing system and a heelclip for extra stability. The bright colour pops and rugged materials represented the hustlers and streetballers who wore them back in the 80s.

Born and bred in New York City, the entrepreneurial designer twins Dee & Ricky then collaborated with Pony in 2012 on a limited edition version of the M100 (three of which are shown here), releasing it on the boys' 26th birthday. Dee & Ricky's usual flamboyant bright colour blocking together with a mix of premium materials such as leather, suede, 3M, ballistic nylon, wool and patent leather, made sure that this 80s gem was brought right up to date.

SHOE DATA

EDITION
Dee & Ricky
YEAR RELEASED
2012
ORIGINAL PURPOSE
Basketball
TECHNOLOGY
**Micro-pillow heel;
ventilation holes;
Hytrel ankle
support system;
ghillie lacing**

COLLABORATORS

Collaborations can turn even the most obscure sneakers into objects of desire. The story behind the shoe adds weight to every colour choice, material application or modification that together make up the unique package.

It takes a brand with a strong history and ethos to produce a successful and well-executed limited release that will go down in sneaker history. Once a brand and a partner make an impact with their first collaboration, chances are that is not the last you will see of them. Patta is a prime example of this, with its abundance of Nike Air Max interpretations.

Key collaborators, such as the HTM collective (one of Nike's longest-running partners), have developed their own following. Having first made an impression with a design for the classic Air Force 1 in 2002, today HTM are the 'go to' all stars who introduce Nike's innovations – they manage to turn an unknown concept into a wearable collectable. Crooked Tongues and Footpatrol are also highly regarded collaborators whose designs have stood

the test of time. Having worked with most of the leading brands over the years, their wealth of sneaker knowledge has allowed them to bring the consumer connoisseur's perspective to their collaborations. Often looking back at heritage silhouettes and colourways for inspiration, they pay extra-special attention to every panelled detail, never scrimping on quality and sometimes offering more than just sneakers for your buck.

In this section we take an in-depth look at some of the most featured collaborators, explaining a little more about their brands, their histories and the stories behind their sneakers – how they became iconic, and what drives them forward.

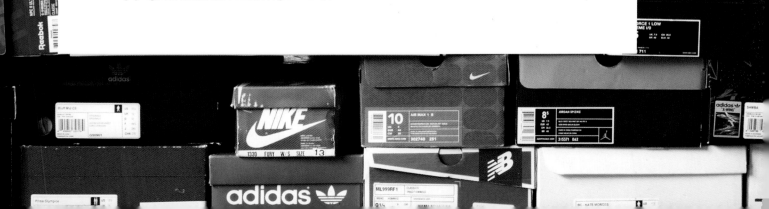

Nike HTM

HIROSHI TINKER MARK

When three sneaker luminaries – Hiroshi Fujiwara (Fragment Design), Tinker Hatfield (Nike's vice president for design and special projects) and Mark Parker (Nike CEO and designer) – joined forces to form the HTM collective in the early noughties, a special partnership was born.

The trio had a lifetime of sneaker industry experience between them, and this knowledge paved the way for a new approach to sneaker design. HTM work together organically, which gives them the freedom to design the best possible products without the restraints of rules or time limits. This open-minded collaborative approach has led to some unique and game-changing shoes.

HTM like to surprise. They push the boundaries of conventions in the use of fabric, colour and pattern and, as such, challenge notions of performance and style. Usually the first to work on Nike's inspirational new technologies and silhouettes, for instance the Nike Air Woven (pages 110–11), or the Nike HTM Flyknit (pages 152), HTM have created aesthetically outstanding trainers that have essential cutting-edge technology at their core.

As a result, HTM products are always highly desirable. The HTM partnership is collaboration at its best.

MISTER CARTOON

Mark Machado earned his nickname, Mr Cartoon, through his art. Starting out from an early age airbrushing T-shirts and low-riders, he quickly became known as a graffiti artist. After hanging out in tattoo shops, he naturally progressed into the world of ink and developed a style for which he is now notorious, in the medium of fine line tattooing, which was invented in the Californian prison system.

Embraced by the world of hip-hop, Mr Cartoon's work has featured in magazines, music videos and CD covers for rappers such as Cypress Hill, and his ink is marked onto the skin of many celebrities. The busy artist also runs Joker Brand Clothing with fellow Mexican-American sneaker lover Estevan Oriol, his own marketing company called SA studio, and a car-care product company, Sanctiond Automotive.

Mr Cartoon's style and influence led to his first sneaker collaboration on the hip-hop favourite Nike Air Force 1. He went on to apply his fine line style to more Air Force 1s, and has also worked closely with Vans on many projects. To date, he has done eight sneaker collaborations.

dave White

Dave White is a renowned British artist who has been exhibiting for over twenty years. Often influenced by popular culture, White's work is uniquely expressive and vibrant. His designs have broad appeal, and as a result he has collaborated with brands ranging from AOL to Coca-Cola and Converse.

Since 2002 White has been especially known for pioneering the 'sneaker art' movement, developing a 'wet paint' style. White created oil-on-canvas paintings of classic Nike and Jordan Brand models that were exhibited globally to great acclaim.

The year 2005 saw the collaborative relationship with Nike continue with the 'Neon Pack' (page 125), which really brought home the art of sneaker design, and in 2011 White collaborated on the Jordan Brand charitable project WINGS for the Future (pages 172–73), designing twenty-three pairs of bespoke trainers that were auctioned off to raise over $23,000. It's no surprise that when the Dave White x Air Jordan I saw a general release in 2012, it was one of the most hyped trainers of that year.

RONNIE FIEG

Ronnie Fieg is a New York-based designer, born and raised in Queens, who has been entrenched in footwear culture his whole life. Working his way up from stockboy to buyer in David Z stores in Manhattan, Fieg gained a vast knowledge (and collection) of sneakers, which inspired him to go on and create his own.

Fieg first collaborated with a brand in 2007 when he designed five ASICS Gel-Lyte III colourways. The range was a success, with all 252 pairs selling in one day. Fieg went on to collaborations with ASICS and a whole host of other brands: adidas, Clarks, Converse, Herschel Supply Co., New Balance, Polo Ralph Lauren, Puma, Red Wing Shoes, Saucony…the list goes on!

In 2011 Fieg opened his own streetwear store, KITH NYC, which stocks many of the same brands he has collaborated with and often releases his collaborations exclusively. Fieg's knowledge of what makes a trainer good is arguably unparalleled, as are his interpretations of a range of classic products.

In the Granite City – namely, Aberdeen – is Hanon Shop, renowned for its rare and classic kicks, as well as a collection of stylish apparel. It has been in the trade since 1990 and has a reputation as one of the best boutiques in the UK, with a vast amount of stock available online.

Collaborating with many of the big names, such as New Balance, Saucony and adidas, to name a few, Hanon Shop's team have introduced a common thread into most

of their designs. Being fiercely proud of their city, they have Scottish culture, material and even weather reference points on their shoes. Their local running club colourway inspired the ASICS 'Wildcats' Gel-Lyte III (page 53).

Although Hanon Shop's work embodies an old-school design aesthetic, the use of materials and technology always comes with a fresh perspective.

Founders Michael Kopelman, Simon Porter and Fraser Cooke first opened Footpatrol's doors in the heart of Soho back in 2002. Quickly gaining notoriety for stocking some of the most sought-after streetwear around – including Japanese exclusives and rare deadstock – Footpatrol soon became the number one spot for London's sneaker enthusiasts to hang out.

After closing in 2008, Footpatrol was gladly welcomed back in 2010 when

it reopened in a new Berwick Street location, now owned and managed by JD Sports (Pentland Group). The design of the store was inspired by the tiny boutiques of Japan and it contains an intimate-feeling 'second' shop complete with pitched roof. The materials that make up the store interior are unapologetically basic yet sturdy and, as such, they reflect Footpatrol's ethos when it comes to making sneakers: practicality and design are seamlessly fused together. This holds

true just as much under the JD umbrella as it did before. Notably, Footpatrol drew inspiration from the natural materials in tne shop for the much-heralded Footpatrol x ASICS Gel-Saga II (page 58) in 2012.

Footpatrol's signature gas mask logo can be found on a fair few releases contained in these pages.

A BATHING APE

The million-dollar brand A Bathing Ape (BAPE) is a Japanese streetwear label that has opened stores throughout Japan, Asia, London, Paris and New York, later expanding to BAPE Cuts hair salon, BAPE Sounds records, BAPE Café and gallery.

Founder Nigo referenced the cult film *Planet of the Apes* when he chose the famous ape head logo and name in 1993. The phrase 'A Bathing Ape in Lukewarm Water', which refers to a spoilt generation of Japanese youths indulging in warm baths, the type of people who would become avid BAPE consumers, is also said to have been a key influence on the name.

Starting with T-shirts, hoodies, jeans and jackets, BAPE soon went on to produce its own footwear, the Bapesta, which was inspired by Nike's Air Force 1, while also collaborating with key sportswear brands on silhouettes such as the now-infamous adidas Superstars and Campus. All BAPE products are produced in small runs, meaning the exclusive designs often sell out quickly and cause mass queues around the world.

In 2011 BAPE was sold to Hong Kong fashion giant I.T, which bought a 90 per cent stake in the company for nearly $3 million. Nigo agreed to remain creative director of the brand for the first few years.

Shawn Stüssy founded the eponymous surfwear company – now world famous, and one of California's longest-established clothing brands – in 1984 in conjunction with his friend Frank Sinatra Jr.

The iconic logo came into being when Shawn scrawled his name onto handcrafted surfboards with a marker pen. He later transferred the logo to T-shirts and caps that he sold from his car boot. The surfwear trend was soon adopted by skate, punk, hip-hop and other street-oriented subcultures.

The brand has grown substantially and now has 'Chapter' stores situated in almost every continent. After more than thirty years, Stüssy continues to release sought-after limited edition products.

In 2000 Stüssy bagged its first sneaker collaboration with Nike, when UK distributor Michael Kopelman and Nike's Fraser Cooke (who went on to found Footpatrol) worked together on the Air Huarache. Many subsequent releases have included the friends and family Air Huarache Light, which was the first Nike sneaker to feature another brand name on it (page 101). Stüssy has gone on to successfully collaborate with Converse, Vans and adidas alongside its seminal work with Nike.

Supreme

Supreme first opened its doors in 1994 on Lafayette Street in downtown Manhattan, founded by James Jebbia. The brand is now known around the world. Its iconic logo, based on Barbara Kruger's propaganda art, made the Futura Heavy Oblique font synonymous with skate and street culture.

Stemming from a group of skaters and artists, who also make up Supreme's store staff, crew and customers, the brand's core ethos has always been about the downtown culture. Working and collaborating with some of the world's leading designers, artists, photographers and musicians, such as Terry Richardson, Jeff Koons, Raekwon and Lady Gaga, Supreme has stayed current and always relevant, distributing worldwide and opening stores throughout Japan and London.

Its skate background has made Supreme a key collaborator with Nike SB and Vans. It has played a key part in the evolution of some of Nike's most iconic models – for example, Supreme initiated the development of the Zoom Bruin SB and Air Trainer II SB. Its application of Pop art, and ability to bring together influential artists and musicians to create highly desirable Vans silhouettes, has led to some of the most successful collaborations of all time.

UNDEFEATED

Two like-minded affiliates opened their first Undefeated store in 2001. James Bond and Eddie Cruz, both self-confessed sports nerds, also shared a passion for art, music and fashion. They brought all of these interests together when they opened Undefeated.

Having started in Los Angeles, Undefeated now boasts stores across the United States and Japan, with distribution spanning most of the world, specializing in sport-specific streetwear in limited runs. Its distinctive Five Strikes logo is reminiscent of how players keep score on the streets.

This premium brand likes to give back to the community by sponsoring sporting events and parties. The billboard above the LA store is sponsored by Nike and, rather than advertising, the shop displays works by various artists such as Geoff McFetridge, KAWS, José Parlá and Kehinde Wiley.

Undefeated is deep in the game of sneaker collaborations, having worked with adidas, New Balance, Nike, Puma, Reebok and Vans. From 2001 it has explored an assortment of colour and material combinations, ranging from practically simple to outrageously complex. The well-respected executions always receive an overwhelming response.

mita sneakers

In the middle of downtown Tokyo, in the district of Ueno, lives the well-established and renowned store Mita Sneakers.

Starting as a traditional Japanese shoe shop selling *geta* and *waraji*, it was originally known as Mita Shoten; with current owner Kozaburo Mita's forward-thinking vision, the focus turned to selling

sneakers. The sneaker boom of the 90s, coupled with Mita's vast and unique selection, enabled it to become one of the most prominent boutiques in the area.

Since then, Mita Sneakers' creative director, Shigeyuki Kunii, has collaborated with many brands over the years, bringing exclusive releases to sneaker enthusiasts worldwide.

The store's wire-fencing wall design is often used as a signature print on the innersoles of Mita's collaborations.

CLOT

In 2003 childhood friends Edison Chen and Kevin Poon set up Hong Kong-based streetwear brand CLOT, which rapidly gained a reputation for stocking on-point lifestyle goods. Almost inevitably, given the creative minds of its co-founders, CLOT launched its own line of products in 2004 and they have flown off the shelves ever since. This led to the launch of

renowned designer streetwear store JUICE in major Asian cities such as Hong Kong, Shanghai, Taipei and Kuala Lumpur.

Over the years the brand has grown from music and fashion to design services, PR consulting and even event organization. The CLOT label promotes collaboration between Eastern and Western youth culture styles and

this stance is key to its sneaker collaborations with a notable list of international brands, including Kanye West, Disney, Lacoste, adidas, Nike, Converse and Vans.

In 2006 the iconic Air Max 1 'Kiss of Death' (page 115) collaboration with Nike hit the shelves. The shoe was inspired by Chinese medicine. Not only did it have sneakerheads raving, but it also marked the first ever collaboration between Nike and a Hong Kong-based label.

variety of footwear, as well as apparel, accessories and, of course, Patta's in-house brand.

Out of love and necessity, rather than profit and novelty, the Patta store opened its doors at the Nieuwezijds Voorburgwal in 2004. Sited in the heart of Amsterdam, the store became the centre of attention by bringing new excitement to the Dutch scene. Within a relatively short time Patta went from importing footwear from overseas, to being rewarded with the top-tier accounts from all of its favourite brands, to collaborating with them on products, resulting in Amsterdam's true one-stop shop and platform for streetwear culture.

After eight years at the original location, Patta relocated to the historical Zeedijk, offering the familiar Patta vibe, yet with a new look and feel to communicate the Patta image. The retail space is designed to showcase the store's

Aside from footwear staples such as Nike, adidas, Converse, ASICS, Reebok, KangaROOS, New Balance and UBIQ, they also stock clothing brands including Stüssy, Rockwell, Kangol and Norse Projects. More ideas, concepts, products and collaborations with various brands are soon to follow, as growth and expansion continue…

SNEAKERSNSTUFF

Putting Sweden on the map as a top sneaker location is Sneakersnstuff, with two stores – in Stockholm and Malmö – as well as a strong online presence.

Owners Erik Fagerlind and Peter Jansson, avid collectors before they opened the store in 1999, were keen to make exclusive sneakers available in Sweden, just as their friends had done Stateside. Of course, along with hard-to-find and premium sneakers, they also stock the

much-loved classics. Sneakersnstuff has collaborated with a number of brands over the years, including adidas, Reebok, New Balance and Converse, and, in true Scandinavian style, many of the designs are minimal in tone and all about unusual textures and fabrics. Super-soft animal skins and wool, both highly functional and downright good looking, have been used frequently. The understated Sneakersnstuff 'SNS' logo is most often subtly called out on the shoe.

What started as a bunch of like-minded people gathering outside a shop bench in London became one of the world's biggest sneaker sites and forums, Crooked Tongues (CT). Owner Russell Williamson and his friends successfully turned an obsession into their bread and butter in 2000, as the website became one of the most reliable resources of sneaker news, a place where fans could express their excitement (and gripes) over releases, and an online store carrying the classics, rare vintages and other sought-after designs. CT has since become known for its legendary annual BBQ event, even venturing as far afield as Thailand for the annual blowout.

What sets this store apart from the others is its honest approach. The site's opinion-led features don't favour just the shoes stocked on the webstore, so integrity abounds; this honesty follows through into the collaborations too, with inspirations ranging from archive colourways to the CT online forum.

Over the years, CT has partnered up with many footwear brands and created some stellar sneakers, such as the one-off New Balance x House 33 x Crooked Tongues (page 87), which features an all-over, eye-catching signature House 33 print on premium leather.

German boutique and online retailer Solebox is one of the world's most influential sneaker destinations, having catered to those seeking rare models for over a decade now. The physical store is located in Berlin and houses not just a huge array of footwear, but clothing, accessories and magazines too.

The store has seen a number of makeovers, going from a stark white interior to black walls, but it is the stellar shoe stock that always stands out.

Store owner Hikmet and Co. has collaborated with a number of brands over the years, creating successful New Balance editions, several Reebok releases and some classic adidas designs, to name a few.

solebox®

BEN DRURY

British designer, typographer and illustrator Ben Drury stepped straight into the creative seat at Mo' Wax record label, alongside Will Bankhead, after graduating from Central Saint Martins College of Art and Design in London. The two art directors worked together with Mo' Wax founder James Lavelle to develop iconic artwork for album covers and packaging,

which then led to books, films, toys and clothing. The infamous Nike 'Dunkle' (page 147) took its design and its name from the album *Never, Never, Land* by U.N.K.L.E., on which Drury and Bankhead worked together with graffiti artist Futura.

After Mo' Wax, Drury went on to set up his own design studio in 2000 and continued to collaborate with leading brands Nike and Converse. He tends to combine influences of music, street and fashion culture into his designs. For his first solo collaboration with Nike, Drury was asked to rework an

Air Max 1 around the theme of 'Air', and decided to use pirate radio stations being 'on air' as inspiration (page 123). The result was an instant success. The long-standing relationship between Nike, Ben Drury and Dizzee Rascal led to 2009's Air Max 90, released to coincide with Dizzee's *Tongue N' Cheek* LP, for which Drury created the artwork (page 118).

BODEGA

Jay Gordon, Oliver Mak and Dan Natola wanted to shake things up a little in the heart of Puritan-influenced Boston, so in 2006 they opened a store with a difference. They were inspired by a Spanish trend of the 70s, in which people would steal items from luxury brands, replace the labels and sell them on as their own. The idea of hijacking formed the basis of the store's concept.

The Spanish word *bodega* refers to the convenience store at the front of the shop, which sells all kinds of household products, from pickled eggs to canned

goods and washing detergent. Hidden behind this deceptive front is a land of luxury streetwear, stocking not only Bodega's own line of clothing but also Stüssy, Penfield and Garbstore.

With customers ranging from old ladies buying their washing detergent to kids looking for their next exclusive pair of sneakers, Bodega brought a valuable edge to Boston. The hype led to a range of successful collaborations with Converse, Nike, Vans and Saucony.

ANATOMY OF A SNEAKER

DON'T KNOW YOUR MIDSOLE FROM YOUR MEDIAL? THE ANATOMY OF A SNEAKER CAN BE A COMPLICATED THING, ESPECIALLY AS THE SHOES COME IN DIFFERENT SHAPES AND SIZES FOR VARIED PURPOSES. ESSENTIALLY, MOST SNEAKERS ARE MADE OF THE SAME BASIC PARTS. HERE'S THE SHOE JARGON EXPLAINED, ALONG WITH A TECHNICAL GLOSSARY ON PAGE 252, WHICH HAS GROWN SIGNIFICANTLY SINCE THE FIRST GUIDE.

1. TOE BOX
The toe box is usually made from leather or suede and can be perforated or not. Typically, a runner's toe box is made from nylon mesh for breathability.

2. MIDSOLE
The midsole can be found between the outsole and upper, and is often adorned with branding, print, embossing and the like, but its main function is actually very important – this is where much of the sneaker's cushioning technology is applied.

3. OUTSOLE
These vary in treading brand-by-brand and also depend on the purpose of the shoe. Hard-wearing rubber is the most common material used. This part of the shoe is either stitched or bonded to the upper.

4. FOXING
The foxing is the piece of rubber that joins the upper to the sole.

5. FOREFOOT
Found at the bottom of the shoe, where the ball of the foot is, the forefoot is usually made with flexibility in mind, and with grooves for ease of movement.

6. HEEL
Found at the bottom of the shoe at the rear of the foot. Cushioning is very important here.

7. EYELETS/EYE STAYS
There are two possible uses for eyelets – speed lacing or added stability.

8. INNERSOLE/INSOLE/SOCKLINER/FOOT BED
This is tucked away inside the shoe (usually removable) and contains a heel cup and arch support, providing stability for the foot. A sockliner is the perfect canvas for designs, logos and motifs. Often made of PU foam.

9. TONGUE
The tongue acts as support and provides the foot with a custom fit.

10. SHOE LACES
As we all know, these hold the shoe in place. Most shoe laces on sneakers are made from synthetic fibres or cotton, but they can also be made out of leather, hemp and more.

11. AGLETS
At the tip of the shoe lace, that little piece that keeps the lace from fraying is called the aglet. It is normally made from plastic but is occasionally made special with metal.

12. HEEL PATCH
Prime space for branding.

13. HEEL COUNTER/SIDE PANEL
This wraps around the back of the shoe to the sides, and is used to stiffen the area around the foot for more support.

14. MEDIAL
The medial is the arch side of the shoe.

15. LATERAL
The opposite side to the medial; this is the side that faces outward.

16. LINING
The inside of the upper; manufacturers aim to make the lining soft and breathable, as it has direct contact with the foot or sock.

17. ANKLE COLLAR/ANKLE SUPPORT
The ankle collar is reinforced or padded for comfort or support. This is even more important for high-top shoes.

18. UPPER
The sum of all its parts, the upper groups together everything that isn't the midsole or outsole and generally features a mix of different materials, from suede and leather to nylon mesh and faux animal skins.

19. LACE JEWEL
Some sneakers may have a metal or plastic decorative feature that sits at the bottom of the laces, usually adorned with branding.

20. LOOP TAG
The loop tag isn't a necessity but can be found either wrapped around the tongue to display a logo, or at the heeltab sticking out and acting like a shoehorn; placed here, it is easier to put on the shoe without crushing down the heel collar.

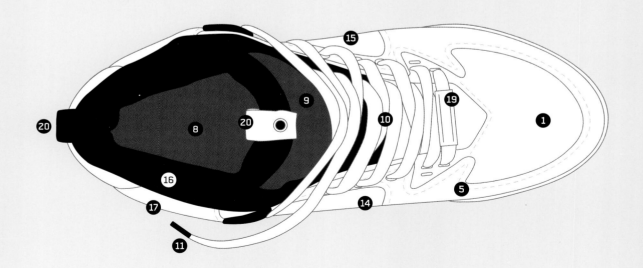

TECHNICAL GLOSSARY

3M SCOTCHLITE
A reflective trim used to enhance visibility at night.

BELLOWS
Also known as a gusseted tongue: the tongue is attached to the outer sides of the sneaker to prevent snow or rain from entering the shoe.

BLOWN RUBBER
An outsole material injected with air, which makes it 40 per cent lighter than standard rubber. Extremely flexible, soft and light.

DUAL-DENSITY EVA MIDSOLE
Midsole made using EVA with double the density, which makes it stronger and firmer.

EVA (ETHYL VINYL ACETATE)
A lightweight material used in the midsole for extra cushioning and shock absorption. When compressed into a pressurized mould, it forms a skin that adds to its durability.

GHILLIE LACING
Lace loops, often D-shaped, that help to provide a comfortable fit. Good for fast lacing.

GUM SOLE
Softer and more flexible than conventional rubber, with added grip. Doesn't mark indoor courts.

HERRINGBONE SOLE
A chevron pattern used on the outsole for good grip and traction.

HOOK-AND-LOOP ANKLE STRAP
Velcro strap usually placed around the ankle to provide further protection, security and stability.

LASER
Etching done by laser machines that burn vector designs onto the shoe's upper.

LED LIGHT
Light-emitting diode increases the visibility and therefore safety of the wearer at night.

ONE-PIECE UPPER
This is an extremely lightweight upper, as there are fewer panels. No stitch lines, which reduces friction between foot and sneaker.

PIVOT POINT
A circular point found on the sole of the foot that aids spinning or pivoting on the courts.

PU (POLYURETHANE) SOLE
Light but highly abrasive outsole unit often used on running and training shoes in the 80s, which increases flexibility, shock absorption and traction.

THINSULATE
Thermal insulation technology that uses synthetic fibre for heat flow and to allow moisture to escape.

TOE GUARD
Usually made of rubber: a cap that protects the toes when manoeuvring on the court.

TPU (THERMOPLASTIC URETHANE)
A lightweight and durable plastic that can be adjusted for the desired level of stiffness, and can be used to make plates that stabilize the shoe.

VULCANIZED SOLE
Vulcanizing involves curing the rubber of the sole and/or foxing with heat to the upper. More durable than regular rubber; can be bent and flexed without losing their original shape.

ADIDAS

ADIZERO
Lightweight construction.

CRISS-CROSS ONE-PIECE ANKLE BRACING SYSTEM
Found on the outer side panel in the shape of an 'X' and enhanced with a hook-and-loop Velcro strap, this provides ankle armour, security and stability.

DELLINGER WEB MIDSOLE
Polyamide web netting covers the midsole from heel to toe, compressing on heelstrike and acting much like a torsion bar.

DUAL-DENSITY POLYURETHANE SOLE
Super-lightweight sole.

EQUIPMENT (EQT)
A range that was introduced in the 90s, offering athletes assorted models for support, cushioning and guidance.

MULTI-DISC
Wide-grip outer sole made up of numerous Trefoil logo discs that form grip cups for improved traction. The serrated edges also help traction and provide shock absorption.

PRIMEKNIT
Fine-tuned knitted yarn, developed for lightweight flexibility and support, with a seamless finish.

SHELL TOE
Durable rubber toe cap that protects the forefoot and assists stop-start motion.

SOFT CELL
Used in the majority of adidas running shoes; developed to improve suspension.

SUCTION CUPS
These provide better traction.

TORSION
Supports the midfoot, providing extended control, fit or protection.

TPU HEEL COUNTER
Adds stability and aids wearers with motion control problems.

ASICS

GEL CUSHIONING SYSTEM
Exclusive silicone-based gel technology is strategically placed at high-impact areas of the midsole, providing optimum shock absorption without sacrificing stability.

SPLIT TONGUE
Eradicates the discomfort created by conventional tongues that slide while running.

STICKY SOLE
Provides extra grip and mobility on the basketball court.

NEW BALANCE

ABZORB
Cushioning in the midfoot that provides exceptional shock absorption.

C-CAP
Compression-moulded EVA used in the midsole that provides cushioning and flexibility.

ENCAP
Blown rubber saturated with air molecules and designed to disperse shock.

ROLLBAR
TPU posting system that minimizes rear-foot movement and controls pronation – vital in motion control/stability running shoes.

NIKE/JORDAN

ACG (ALL CONDITIONS GEAR)
Refers to Nike's outdoor training shoes; differentiated from other lines with the ACG logo.

AIR 180
An Air unit that is visible from 180 degrees with a visible protected unit on the outsole.

AIR MAX 90 CURRENT
This is half an Air Max 90 unit, used to cushion the heel, combined with Air Current sole technology that allows the forefoot to flex freely.

BRS 1000
Long-lasting synthetic rubber used on outsoles. Carbon is added to the rubber.

CLIMA-FIT
Material made from yarn that is tightly woven to be breathable, windproof and water resistant; primarily used on Nike technical clothing.

DURALON
Usually found on the forefoot of a running shoe, made from lightweight, synthetic and porous rubber.

DYNAMIC SUPPORT
A form of cushioning that sits in the midsole and provides support to runners.

FLYKNIT
One-piece upper made up of knitted yarns and fabric variations that are precisely engineered to make a lightweight, form-fitting and almost seamless upper.

FLYWIRE
Strategically placed filaments that offer support; super-light. Paper-thin fabric covers the top of the foot. The Flywire filaments are attached to the outsole and different parts of the upper to hold the foot in place.

FOAMPOSITE
Liquid foam is poured into a synthetic upper and solidifies, creating a moulded upper.

FOOTBRIDGE
Designed for runners. Slows down rolling motion with five stability fingers and two rigid columns along the inside of the shoe. Footbridge was featured on the Air Stab.

FOOTSCAPE
Specially formed sole made to support a wider foot.

FREE
A sole that features deep teeth-like slices to encourage flexibility and extension in both directions. Free shoes are measured on a scale of 0.0 to 10.0, with 0.0 representing a barefoot feel and 10.0 closer to the feel of a traditional running shoe.

HUARACHE
An exposed sock made from perforated neoprene and double-sided lycra. Holds the wearer's foot more efficiently and reduces the risk of injury.

ION-MASK
Liquid repellent nano-coating technology produced by P2i that gives the whole sneaker the best all-round water repellency.

LUNARLITE
Foam used on the midsole that is springy on the foot; even lighter than Phylon. Reduces painful pressure points on the wearer's foot.

LUNARLON
Cushioning that features a soft but tough foam core encased within a supportive foam. Its springy response and lightness help to reduce pressure on the foot.

MAX AIR
A form of Nike Air cushioning that contains maximum air volume for maximum impact protection. Always visible in the midsole.

MOIRE
An almost stitch-free upper with maximum breathability.

NIKE+
Connects shoes to Apple devices, allowing users to track runs, monitor performance and communicate with other runners.

NIKE AIR
Nike Air cushioning provides a comfortable ride. Nike Air is almost always encapsulated in the midsole or sockliner. Original Nike cushioning technology debuted in 1979.

NO-SEW
Seams are pressure welded to create a streamlined sneaker with increased water resistance.

PHYLON
Used in midsoles; more lightweight and resilient than other midsole foams. It is non-yellowing and is resistant to moisture.

PRESTO CAGE
A lacing system that extends to the sides of the Presto, giving more support to the wearer.

TORCH
A seamless three-layer system that allows moisture to leave the shoe, for increased comfort over a longer duration.

VISIBLE AIR
An air unit that is always visible in the midsole.

WOVEN
A woven upper that is a mix of nylon elasticated and non-elastic strands. Elasticated strands are positioned where strength and support are needed.

ZOOM AIR
Super-responsive cushioning that responds to the stress generated by the shoe's wearer, absorbing it and refracting the same stress. Comes in a flat, thin unit.

PONY

HYTREL ANKLE SUPPORT SYSTEM
An integrated support system that delivers an anatomical fit around the ankle and tendon area.

MICRO-PILLOW HEEL
Pony's shock-absorbing cushioning system.

PUMA

DISC
Closure system that increases stability. When the wearer tightens the disc, the internal wires tighten the upper.

ECOORTHOLITE
An eco-friendly insole made from a clean renewable source. Benefits include breathability, moisture control, anti-microbial properties and long-term cushioning.

EVERRIDE
A blown rubber compound providing added cushioning throughout the outsole, while reducing overall shoe weight.

EVERTRACK
A rubber compound with high-abrasion-wear characteristics for durability.

FAAS BIORIDE
Technology comprising three biomechanical, performance-enhancing parts – Rocker, Flex and Groove – that work together to create a naturally responsive shoe. The number reflects the 'Faas Scale': a higher figure indicates more cushioning.

KMS LITE
Innovative midsole material; lighter than standard PUMA EVA soles.

LACE COVER/FLIP TONGUE
Keeps laces out of the way to increase safety for cyclists.

TRINOMIC
Running technology with signature hexagonal graphics; provides exceptional motion control.

REEBOK

3D ULTRALITE
Injection-moulded lightweight foam material that is extra-durable and responsive.

ERS (ENERGY RETURN SYSTEM)
Cylinders made out of plastic DuPont Hytrel embedded into the midsole to act as springs.

HEXALITE
Replacing ERS technology, Hexalite honeycomb-shaped cushioning enhances shock absorption in areas of peak pressure, while being extremely durable.

PU FOAM INSOLE
Absorbs a certain amount of shock on impact, providing extra cushioning for the foot, on top of the midsole cushioning.

PUMP
Internal inflation system: an air chamber surrounding the wearer's foot provides a custom fit. The air is pumped at the tongue.

SAUCONY

XT600 RUBBER OUTSOLE
Carbon rubber, usually placed only on impact points or the triangular lugs of the outsole. It is highly durable and has outstanding abrasion and traction properties.

VANS

DRI-LEX
A perspiration management system made of two layers that pulls moisture from the skin and pushes it to the outer layer to dry quickly.

POWER TRANSFER SOLE
A Power Transfer plate is housed underneath an EVA insole to add stiffness to give a firmer performance.

WAFFLE CUPSOLE
Providing the best of both worlds for skaters: a good-grip vulcanized sole that contains a cup for extra support and protection.

WAFFLE SOLE
An inverted grip sole that gives good traction.

ACKNOWLEDGMENTS

SPECIAL THANKS GO OUT TO EVERYONE WHO PARTICIPATED AND MADE THIS BOOK HAPPEN.

HEAD OF PRODUCTION

Niranjela Karunatilake at U-Dox Creative

DESIGN LEAD

Nick Hearne at U-Dox Creative

PHOTOGRAPHY

Phil Aylen at U-Dox Creative, except:

Ronnie Fieg x ASICS images by KITH NYC, pp. 49–51
Footpatrol store images by Louise Melchior, p. 243

U-DOX TEAM

Phil Aylen, Jess Ayles, Jaymz Campbell, Dan Canyon, Charlie Dennington, James Else, Chris George, Nick Hearne, Paul Jenkins, Liz Jones, Niranjela Karunatilake, Michael Keen, Leo Marks, Joseph O'Malley, Jess Ruiz, Tara Ryan, Joel Stoddart, Matt Tarr, Seb Thomas, Thuy Tran, Tom Viner, Mark Ward, Russell Williamson, Albert Zaragoza

THANKS TO

Mubi Ali, Steve Bryden, Russell Williamson, Niranjela Karunatilake, Chris George, James Else, Chris Aylen, Joel Stoddart, Koba, Waseem Sarwar, Wesley Tyerman, Stevey Ryder, Paolo Caletti, Alex Grant, Glen Flurry, Sunil Rao, Thor Geraldsson, Ayodeji Jegede, David Taylor, Kendra Lee Smith, Rob Stewart, Mark Watson, Blair Massari, Acyde, Justin Ip, Dan Richmond, Bert McLean, Jade Ampofo, Shun Ame Sugimoto, Joseph O'Malley

Masahiro Usui – ABC Mart
Emily Chang, Daniel Bauer, Otto Christian, Olivia Fernandez Marin – adidas
Oliver Mak – Bodega
Hunter and Mr Cartoon
Kevin Poon, Jymi, Pat and all at CLOT
C_LAW, Jei Morris, James Thome – Converse
Dave White – Dave White Studio
Ben Drury
John Brotherhood – Footpatrol
Richard Airey, Mary-Jane Chow – Gimme 5
David Taylor, Dugald Allan – Hanon Shop
Eugene Kan, Kevin Ma – Hypebeast
Corey Kamenoff – KITH NYC
Shigeyuki Kunii and all at Mita Sneakers
Julian Howkins, Adrian Fenech, Jaime McCall,

Ryan Greenwood, Sharmadean Reid, Kristjan Gilles – Nike Sportswear
Annoushka Giltsoff, Sarah Lawson – A Number Of Names
James Nuttall – oki-ni
Gee, Masta Lee – Patta
Aman Tak, Victoria Barrio – Office/Offspring
Mister lego – Pony/Orange Dot
Emma Roach, Ryan Knight – Collective Brands/PRO-Keds
Laura Fairweather, Rima Patel, Ilyana Ari – Puma
Jill Gate, Kirsten Pugsley – Reebok
Peter Jansson, Johan Unden – SNS
Hikmet – Solebox
Scott Terpstra, Emmy Coats – Stüssy INC
Angelo B – Supreme
KB Lee, Ian Coates – Undefeated
Charlie Morgan, Chris Overholser, Jan Pochobradsky, Nichole Matthews – Vans

The Butcher Shop – Bethnal Green Road, London
Peter – Brick Lane Bikes, London
Andy Willis – Frontside, Hackney Wick, London
Dee – Hackney City Farm, London
Damian – Hoxton Bar & Kitchen, London
Londonewcastle Project Space – London
Meteor Sports – Bethnal Green Road, London
Sebastian Tarek Bespoke Shoes Studio – London
Shanghai – Dalston, London

INDEX

INDEX